Innocence Unraveled
Surviving a Torn Childhood

Innocence Unraveled
Surviving a Torn Childhood

Debbie Barnett

Copyright

Copyright © 2020 by Debbie Barnett

Innocence Unraveled: Surviving a Torn Childhood is under copyright protection. No part of this book may be used or reproduced in any manner whatsoever without written permission except in the case of brief quotations embodied in critical articles and reviews. Printed in the United States of America. All rights reserved.

Some names and identifying details have been changed to protect the privacy of individuals.

Cover design by: MiblArt
Interior Formatting: Grace Michael
Editing: Shayla Raquel, ShaylaRaquel.com
Published 2020
Printed in the United States of America
ISBN: 978-1-7331680-2-1

Innocence Unraveled: Surviving a Torn Childhood

www.debbiebarnettauthor.com

Disclaimer

The details in this book come from my personal recollection of the past as well as from others who helped me fill in some gaps and details. To the best of my ability, I have tried to weave an accurate account of the events I describe. Exact dialogue with certain people and exact descriptions of certain situations might not be completely accurate. Although the details might not be 100 percent true, my story is.

I have changed the names of most individuals, but not all, to protect the privacy of those involved. I have changed some places and some identifying characteristics to maintain anonymity.

I might have left out some individuals if they had no relevance to my story and might have intentionally left out some details or even added some details to enhance the story.

This memoir contains stories of childhood/teenage sexual abuse. It contains mature content. Discretion is advised.

Dedication

In loving memory of Azzie Mae Johnson, Audrey Korrick, and David Lichter.

With gratitude to Officer Robert Meyerholtz and Cousin Joel Lerman.

Epigraph

There is no greater agony than bearing an untold story inside you.

— Maya Angelou

Table of Contents

Acknowledgments 1
Introduction 3
Chapter 1 7
Chapter 2 27
Chapter 3 41
Chapter 4 55
Chapter 5 75
Chapter 6 87
Chapter 7 105
Chapter 8 113
Chapter 9 135
Chapter 10 145
Chapter 11 167
Chapter 12 189
Chapter 13 203
Chapter 14 221
Chapter 15 231
Epilogue 253
About the Author 263

Acknowledgments

I owe my greatest thanks to my best friend Patricia Bowes who left this world after a courageous battle with cancer. I'm not sure if I would have had the courage or perseverance to share my story with the world had it not been for Patricia's belief and encouragement in my ability to do so.

A big thank you to my five siblings who all helped me fill in missing gaps from my young life.

Introduction

    I lay in the operating room, my eyes full, scanning for a familiar face. The lights blinded me the way the sun does when reflecting off a blanket of freshly fallen snow. My eyeballs thrashed back and forth like a fish trying to free itself from the hook's grasp. I wanted my cold, numb hands and feet to mask the shame that enfolded me and the tears that streamed down my cheeks to wash it all away. I prayed the pain that riddled my fifteen-year-old body would leave as quickly as it came.

    But the pain sharpened, and it brought me back to his master bedroom in all its radiant glory, window curtains matching the flowered bedspread that I lay upon. This stranger, with his swollen belly and deeply creased jowls, stood in front of me. I was naked from the bottom down with just a sheet covering me. I smelled his armpits and wanted to gag. My boyfriend's father was about to perform an abortion on me. I longed to escape. He examined me. I was tense, and my vagina was dry.

As if the abortion wasn't punishment enough, I remembered him saying the unthinkable: "I need to penetrate you before I perform the abortion so you're moist."

I tried to make sense out of what I heard. I whispered under my breath, "This man is going to violate me . . . oh, God, please forgive me." And then the unthinkable happened. He raped me and afterward, he performed the abortion.

"That poor, poor child." Their whispers were barely audible as they worked quickly and feverishly on me, an IV inserted with pain medication moving through my veins. What had I done to myself? Were they pitying me, or was I in some sort of danger?

I shivered furiously—I was helpless and alone as the cold gripped me like a noose slowly tightening around my neck. The sterile smell was revolting. I wanted to unravel this as quickly as the mistakes I'd made in the many knitted pieces I had created over the years. Only this time, there was no do-over. Now, I wished for one person by my side, my sister Laurie, from whom I always sought comfort—the one I relied on for love and guidance. I was too young to go through this alone.

I was groggy from the pain medication that had finally set in. Laurie appeared with a loving look that emanated much sadness. She rubbed my arm and said, "Oh, Debbie, what did you do? You could have come to me." She kissed me on the forehead before they rolled me into the operating room. Holding my hand, the nurse said, "Count backward starting at ten."

As I did, I slipped into unconsciousness.

Chapter 1

The leaves danced through the gentle breeze in New Haven, Connecticut, their exquisite shades of orange, pink, and magenta fading into each other as they fell to the ground. Summer had parted, making way for the cooler nights, giving glimpses of the long winter ahead. But the only thing on my mind that day was seventh grade.

It was 1967, a year of many firsts. Lyndon B. Johnson was president and tried to assure the American people that we were winning the Vietnam War, but it was no use. Skepticism had crept into the hearts and minds of the American people and had now become a collective Mr. Spock eyebrow raise. Young men, nationwide, burned their draft cards in defiance, and aggressive protests broke out, including thousands who gathered for the original Human Be-In at Golden Gate Park in San Francisco, then Los Angeles, and finally Central Park in New York City. Over fifty thousand people marched and rallied at the Pentagon, demanding resolve.

 Gas was thirty-three cents and a first-class postage stamp—so expensive at five cents—was worth it, I figured, to write to a magazine that offered, "You, too, can be part of the Beatles' Sgt. Pepper's Lonely Hearts Club Band fan club!" I leaped, hopped, and whooped with joy at the chance back then. Muhammad Ali had been stripped of his title as the World's Heavyweight Champ. They even sentenced him to prison for five years—which meant he couldn't box anymore—because he refused to go to war, holding morally firm to his religious beliefs.

 Our school district had recently started its process of desegregation, following many years of judicial court hearings that finally determined it was wholly unjust to keep Black and white people separated in the school systems. Despite Brown vs. Board of Education of Topeka in 1954, the landmark Supreme Court ruling where justices unanimously agreed that segregating children in public schools was unconstitutional, it had taken years for the actual process to begin and finish.

 The road to desegregation was paved by many in the preceding years, including the Little Rock Nine, a brave and determined group of nine

Black students who set a precedent when they enrolled at the all-white Central High School in Little Rock, Arkansas, in September 1957. Their struggle to enter the school was not without protest, and the harassment they endured through the first year was unprecedented. To add further malice to an already harrowing situation, in September 1958, the governor of Arkansas closed the doors to all Little Rock Schools to do away with desegregation.

During the absence of an entire school year, the formation of many groups, both for and against desegregation, were formed. Over a twenty-day campaign, which included the firing of many teachers and the recall of three segregationist members, the people of Little Rock had finally come to accept limited desegregation. Finally, on June 18, 1959, a three-judge federal district court declared the closure of Arkansas's schools unconstitutional, and in August of 1959, schools were reopened.

Out of the nine students, only one, Ernest Green, became the first African American to graduate Central High on May 25, 1958. All nine students played an integral part in the Civil Rights Movement, and in 1999, President Clinton awarded each of the Little Rock Nine the Congressional Gold Metal.

10 Innocence Unraveled

The long hurdle had run its crusade between 1954 and 1974 for all public schools to become integrated, and now I was faced with little understanding of how school integration would affect me. I had grown up with my beloved Black nanny, Azzie Mae, so I figured that everything would be okay and maybe even fun.

Thanks to the help of Azzie, I had learned many things—things my mother never taught me. As I stood in front of Dr. Susan S. Sheridan Junior High School, a modest, neo-Gothic-style brick building with a large courtyard in the center of the complex, getting ready to enter the eighth grade, I thought back to the day Azzie taught me how to tie my shoelaces.

With my shoelaces tight on a fall day not unlike this one, I ran around my lawn in circles like a cat chasing its tail, my high-rise suspender skirt swirling as it followed my dance. The sun's warmth tickled my nose. Azzie, with her watchful eye on me, exclaimed, "I'm so proud of you!" Bent over slightly with her arms extended, she motioned for me to run into the folds of her arms. "Baby girl, you did so good!" I don't know that Azzie ever called me Debbie—only Baby Girl.

I dashed toward her, and in one fell swoop, she lifted me. Her embrace was warm and loving, like a protective shield, a feeling I would never forget.

She let me down and said, "Show me how you tie them laces again, Baby Girl." In a frenzy and so eager for her approval, I fumbled to undo the laces on my saddle shoes, causing them to turn into a knotted mess. I stomped my feet in frustration.

"Let me help you with that, Baby Girl. Come here and put your foot up on my leg."

I lifted my foot and placed it on her thigh.

"There you go. Now go ahead and untie the other one. Pull it here from this side so it won't get knotted." Pointing me in the right direction, I undid the other shoelace, and then after tying and untying a few times, I finished. I stood up and poked my chest out and stood as tall as the new building I was about to enter.

Azzie patted me on the head and reaffirmed, "I am so proud of you." With a big grin, she added, "I know in that pretty little blonde head of yours that you can do anything you put your mind to. *You* are a very smart girl."

I beamed with delight.

~ ~ ~

And now I gulped, wondering about my first day at Sheridan.

While I was looking through my backpack in the courtyard at school waiting for the homeroom bell to ring, a group of new students—all Black girls—stared me down. I quickly glanced away and continued rummaging through my things. It didn't deter them. I could feel their eyes on me like a wild animal's intent on its prey. I pretended to delve deeper into my bag, trying to seem busy, as if I were playing *Let's Make a Deal,* and I'd win a prize if I found a ridiculous, random object in there. Maybe a pepper shaker? A walnut cracker? A blender? A magic cape to help me—*poof!*—disappear? For Pete's sake, where was Monty Hall when I needed him?

Still, I could feel their piercing stares. *Uh-oh. This could be trouble.*

There were six of them, huddled and whispering. Suddenly, one girl cackled loudly as she stuck her tongue out. Another girl hissed at me, which sounded like a snake. Now, all of them were staring, menacingly. I frantically searched the grounds to find a teacher or even another student. I wondered and tried to calculate if I could dart past them toward the door that led inside, but they were strategically blocking it. *Oh my God. What's* happening? *Are they going to attack me?* Then, slowly, methodically, they started making their way toward me. One by one, they surrounded me.

One heavier, taller girl, wearing a bright-yellow shirt and green plaid skirt, got within an inch of my face, looked me up and down, blew a bubble with her gum, and cracked it loudly in my ear. I begged myself to be calm and to show no fear, but my lip twitched in betrayal. As the circle closed in on me, the girls began to clap their hands, stomp their feet, and chant in unison, "*Blonde shit, Blonde shit, Blonde shit.*" I was outnumbered, six to one. Their angry eyes saturated my being with unbridled fear. I wanted to run. Hide. The fight-or-flight mechanism took over. I trembled in agonizing trepidation, yet I felt paralyzed.

The more they chanted, the more ferociously I shook. My feet turned inward, awkwardly. As an odd reflex, I grasped my bag even tighter, imagining—for just a millisecond—that it was a magic umbrella. I pictured myself turning into Mary Poppins and my purse turning into an umbrella, lifting me up, up, and away, looking down and yelling, "Bye for now . . . and later!"

But I wasn't Mary Poppins. I was simply a girl they'd picked on to bully. It could have been anyone. My young mind wondered if it was because I was the stereotypical, blonde-haired, blue-eyed girl. *I'm Jewish*, I thought. *And what about Azzie? Surely if you knew of my relationship with Azzie, we'd be friends. Plenty of bigotry to go around. Can't we be friends? I'm not your enemy.*

However, they weren't psychic. They couldn't read my mind, and they hated me. It was nothing I did. It upset me to the core, and it scared me. It saddened me as well because they didn't know about my relationship with Azzie.

Now, one girl pounded her fist as another came so close to me that I could hear teeth grinding. Again, I looked around, desperately, for another soul, anyone to save me. And, in that instant, the homeroom bell rang. The girls chuckled at first and dispersed, one by one, until I was left alone, with a bladder that had almost emptied right there on the courtyard grounds. Luckily, I—and it—were intact, bodily fluids where they should be, and I made a record-time beeline for the door when they were gone. It had been a nightmare, and I hadn't been daydreaming. There was no fake bogeyman under the bed. I needed to get the hell outta Dodge.

Later that day, although hesitant, I decided I was going to tell my mother what happened at school. I was concerned that she might think I was exaggerating. Had Laurie, my older sister by nine years, still been living at home, I would have confided in her. But she had married at nineteen and already had a two-year-old in tow. When she was home, she rallied for all of us kids by keeping things organized and clean. Taking up the slack while Mom was busy socializing, she'd keep an eye on Kenny, my younger brother, and me, ensuring we were clean and dressed appropriately. While Laurie and Azzie both provided me the stability my mother didn't, their roles were very different. Azzie was my security blanket: warm, comforting, nurturing, and loving. She kept me locked up and under her watchful eye. I learned street smarts from Azzie. Laurie was the "somebody has to watch over these kids" sister who made sure we were looked after and well cared for when my mother wasn't around, which was often.

My mother returned home from a day of mah jongg and was already preparing dinner when I approached her in the kitchen. "Mommy . . . today at school, something horrible happened to me." A surge of heat washed over my face.

"Like what?" she asked with hesitation. She never once lifted her head from the mixing bowl.

Why don't you just stick your head in there? My heart rate quickened with that thought, and it seemed to match the rhythm of her hands as they pulsated the meat loaf. I took a deep breath and exhaled out the words: "The Black girls, well…" I began to pace around the kitchen.

"What about the colored girls, Debbie?" She glanced at me out of the corner of her eye. "And, can you please stand still?" She shook her head in annoyance.

I finally blurted out with each sentence colliding into the other, "They bullied me. There were lots of them. They surrounded me and made fun of me. They called me blonde shit. I'm afraid to go back to school tomorrow."

She pointed her index finger at me in a jabbing motion. I thought for a moment that she was getting ready to scold me, but she said, "Well, we aren't going to let those colored people get away with that, are we? Who do they think they are, anyway? I just knew that allowing them in our schools would turn out to be a mess. I'll teach them a lesson. I'll make an appointment to speak to the principal." She let out a loud huff as she abruptly turned away from me and went back to her dinner preparation.

I should have been relieved by her words, and as much as I wanted the harassment to stop, there was a part of me that didn't want them to get in trouble. I was emotionally drained, listening to my mother single them out like criminals, and especially when she said, "Those *colored* people." I knew in my heart she didn't like Black people. I could tell by the way she sometimes treated Azzie.

I gagged on my own saliva, suddenly feeling nauseated. I wanted to defend those girls. Maybe they were just having a bad day.

"Thanks, Mommy," I finally said. I left the kitchen defeated, my shoulders slumped, and my head pointed to the ground as if I were looking for answers on the floor. I should have been elated at my mother's willingness to help me, yet I was defeated. *Is she protecting me, or is she out to get those girls?*

When I stepped into the hallway just outside the kitchen, I heard Azzie's soft voice, as always, waiting to console me.

"Baby Girl, come here," she whispered.

I approached her. She was sitting in the high-back lounge chair in the living room opposite the kitchen. I leaned over her, getting as close as I could, one ear tilted toward her mouth and in a huddle we often made so my mom couldn't hear.

"Now listen here, baby girl. I heard your mama in there. She might not like us colored folk, but at the same time, them colored girls can't be picking on my baby girl."

"Yeah, but . . . even though I was scared to death—and I mean, *scared to death*—I don't want them to get into trouble."

She offered a consoling smile. "I know, I know. That's because you have a caring heart. Don't ever change your ways, Baby Girl. Someday when you're older, you'll fully understand more about why us colored folk are so angry at the white folk all the time. You'll learn all about the Jim Crow era in your history books and how the white man used the Black man as slaves simply because they were born black. Black folk had no say in just about anything they did."

Azzie's eyes widened as she continued. I could detect some sadness and hurt in her voice, and had I not known better, I could swear tears were welling up in her eyes. "Colored folk had to use separate bathrooms, had to sit in the back of the buses, and weren't able to vote. We were treated like animals, Baby Girl. Worse than animals! Why, dogs and cats and cattle were treated more favorably than we were. We were forced to sleep in small, often uncomfortable quarters far from our masters' houses, as if we were quarantined from the rest of the world. If a man didn't obey his master, he was beaten to a pulp. It was sheer terror for colored folk."

I climbed up atop her lap and lay my head against her full bosom, soft and inviting. Azzie continued, "Even though we fought back real hard with the help of some very brave people, especially a woman by the name of Harriet Tubman who risked her life to free over three hundred slaves, we still had a long way to go even after the Civil War put an end to slavery in 1865. We were treated like second-class citizens for almost one hundred years after the war ended, especially women who weren't allowed to vote. But thank-fully, President Johnson signed the Civil Rights Act in 1964, which legally ended discrimination and segregation that had been established by the Jim Crow laws. And, as grateful as we all were for President Johnson's effort, we still had our own very personal battle to work through, as discrimination would leave its indelible mark on the color of our skin and rear its ugly head time and time again."

I lifted my head enough to look Azzie square in the eye and said, still whispering so that Mommy couldn't hear, "So I was right in not wanting them to get into trouble?"

"You were right in having a caring and compassionate heart; however, I tell you about what happened to the colored folk not to excuse those girls that taunted you, but I tell you this stuff so that you understand why they act the way they do. Colored folk are still angry, so we pass that anger down to our children like a family heirloom, assuring we never forget. Those girls need to learn better behavior just as you need to learn why they do what they do. Maybe in another hundred years, things will be even better. Maybe by then, people will see people as fellow human beings rather than judging people by the color of their skin. I know God wouldn't have made any of us by mistake. You understand all this a little better now, Baby Girl?"

I kissed Azzie on her smooth, full cheek. My thoughts escaped from Harriet Tubman and Jim Crow to the softness of her skin which I adored. She had told me her secret to soft skin and no wrinkles was Vaseline. Although she was old, she never knew her birth date or real age. She used November 23 as her birthday, so that was the day we celebrated. I imagined her to be quite old at around forty-five years, and if she looked that good, then I was going to be using that greasy Vaseline too!

"Baby Girl, are you listening to me?"

"Oh, yes, I am. I get it," I said in a start, shifting my thoughts away from Azzie's soft skin. "I never knew all that stuff went on. That is so sad, but I'm happy Harriet Tubman was so brave and that they stopped that Jim Crow person."

Azzie sat back in the chair and let out a full belly laugh, the waves rippling up and down her torso. "Jim Crow isn't a real person, Baby Girl. He was a fake character in a show, who they made out to be a racist during the days of slavery when white folk made all those rules for us and considered us less than human."

I let out an embarrassing sigh and placed my hands on my head. I could feel the heat well up in my cheeks. How silly that must have sounded to her. But what did I know? I was just a twelve-year-old kid. All that stuff she had told me and the gravity of it was just beginning to sink in. Azzie had talked about God many times, but if there was a God, I wondered how he could let all that happen.

~ ~ ~

22 *Innocence Unraveled*

After my talk with Azzie, I was relieved my mother rallied behind me. Rehashing the events from school made me shudder. Even though I was surprised, grateful, and somewhat embarrassed, I was thankful that she spoke to the principal. And it worked. They left me alone. However, that day, I learned a lot. Although I wasn't from any sort of upper-crust white world—quite the opposite—I learned, through Azzie's words, that to those girls and most Black people at the time, their world was indeed Black and white. We didn't have to think about it. Those girls forced me to understand, and I got the message. It was an important one—albeit terrifying—but I'll never forget it. It didn't make me hate Black people; on the contrary, it made me sympathize with their current issues. The system had been rigged and still was. To me, it didn't look like racism, as Azzie called it, was going anywhere, anytime soon.

Although they never tormented me again, I was still traumatized. At times, my fear paralyzed me as I walked around the school grounds. I must have looked like a nervous squirrel, stopping and pausing to see who was coming. I dreaded passing them in the hallways. I figured they'd give me a nasty look or judge my appearance, never wanting to get to know the real me. I wasn't wrong. That's how it went down. I had to get through the rest of the school year unscathed. My mother had decided to send me to New Haven Hebrew Day School, a Jewish religious school for the eighth grade. She thought that a year at private school before sending me back to the public high school might give integration a chance to improve—and it did.

Azzie continued to share her insights with me often, voicing her opinion while paralleling the differences between the white and Black man. I was as eager as a baby grabbing at a toy for the first time, intent to learn more about her. I had wondered about where she lived, in "her neck of the woods," as she called it. I had imagined the differences between there and where I grew up at 83 Curtis Drive, a predominately all-white, Jewish suburb of New Haven.

One day after school, I found Azzie in the basement doing laundry. I listened intently to her words as she transported me into her world and then back to mine as she spoke of the "hood."

"Baby Girl, someday, you gots to come to my neck of the woods."

"Okay. When?" I said, my voice elevated in excitement.

"Ain't nothing like these parts," she muttered while shaking her head from side to side.

"Nope, nothing like these parts. Unlike these streets that gets cleaned with one of them big ole machines, there is trash scattered everywhere on our streets. And the pretty houses here in Westville, well, most of our houses has paint peeling off—could be taken for some new art form."

My eyes widened, and I wrinkled my nose. "Really?" *Gross, dirty streets and peeling paint.* "Tell me more." I stepped closer to Azzie, not wanting to miss any detail.

"So, take summertime. The big folk will be sitting on front stoops or on lawn chairs, just shooting the breeze or playing cards, while the little ones are running around half-naked on dirt-covered lawns. Oh, Lawdy . . . and the dogs are running amok everywhere, barking up a storm."

Azzie smiled, and her initial embarrassment dissipated as she started to hum a tune I was not familiar with. She continued. "And, it ain't unusual to hear a tune blaring from the radio of a lollygagging sixty-seven Cadillac Deville convertible. Those men just love to show off their cars, and what better way to bring attention to them than a radio loud enough to wake a sleeping baby."

Azzie let out a large breath of air, a sign indicating she might be finished with her story.

"More, please." I placed my head against her arm, applying a little nudge as if I could bribe her with affection. I didn't want the story to end.

"That's enough for now, Baby Girl. If I tell you everything, you'll have no reason to come visit me."

I shrugged as she patted the top of my head while the distinct difference to my neighborhood played a picture show in my mind: spotless painted houses, beautiful flower beds, and manicured lawns. A mom sunning herself on a lawn chair while sipping iced tea and watching her progeny play on their plush, carpeted yard.

I let out a long sigh and wrapped my arms as far around her large belly as I could reach. There was something so safe, warm, and inviting about her. I didn't want the story to end. I wanted more because I didn't fully understand. Yet something inside me, plus Azzie's descriptions, made me believe the disparity was wide. From the Jim Crow era to our neighborhood differences—this was a black and white world. My mother was openly racist, yet she trusted Azzie to watch over me. Maybe it was ignorance. Perhaps she never learned about that Jim Crow time or how poorly the white man treated the black man.

Innocence Unraveled

Azzie had opened my eyes to a world I never knew existed. I was just beginning to realize my mother was not alone in her views. It was the norm for most white people, each generation learning from the previous. If this was fact, maybe, just maybe, her being racist was not her fault. And, although it didn't make it right, I had gained an understanding of my mother and what had made those Black girls lash out at me.

Chapter 2

As I did every day, I left the school grounds of Sheridan in a rush, quick to get home to avoid being confronted by those girls. It was a dreary, rainy, bone-chilling February afternoon. Trying to protect my head with my backpack, I hurried toward the bus stop. Miserable and drenched, I dreaded the long walk home after being dropped off. The bus stop was still blocks and blocks away from my house, and the weather simply sucked.

Suddenly a car I didn't recognize pulled up alongside me. As the window slowly rolled down, I saw that it was my history teacher, Mr. Benedetto. He was a slight-framed Italian man with corkscrew curls that fell just above his shoulders. His olive skin revealed his Northern Italian heritage, and he wasn't much taller than I was at five foot seven. He stood out among the other burly teachers because he could pass for one of the students.

He greeted me with a warm smile and kindly asked if I wanted a lift home. "So you don't have to walk in the rain," he added.

A smile crept up my lips. Cop a ride from my teacher? Hm . . . at least I won't have to walk in the downpour and get even more sopping wet. Cool. "That'd be great, Mr. Benedetto." And so, I agreed and got into his car.

Mr. Benedetto drove for about a minute in silence while I listened to my wet sneakers squeak and squish beneath me, drenched from the rain. Then, he spoke. "Debbie, you're a pretty girl and very smart."

I nodded. "Thanks."

"You must have a boyfriend?"

I squirmed in my seat and then shook my head.

He continued: "I can tell that you're a special girl and extremely mature, far beyond your years."

I am! I thought. *At least someone gets it.* "I suppose so."

Mr. Benedetto looked over at me, grinned, and asked, "I was wondering if you'd like to come to dinner at my home? Someday soon? You could meet my wife. She's a fantastic cook. I know she'd love meeting you too."

Lawdy, Lord. I straightened myself up and flipped my long blonde hair behind me and broadened my chest. *I am important and special.* His words lifted me and comforted me as if I were floating high above in the clouds or embraced by the warmth of Azzie's bosom. *Not even a candy apple down at Savin Rock could top this feeling,* I thought, chuckling to myself. Without much hesitation, I replied, "Yes! Yes, sure! I would love to come over. Thanks for the invite."

As we drove the rest of the way, there was silence, yet I was smiling fiercely inside. My teacher thought I was beautiful, special, and even smart. Those words were never uttered at home unless by Azzie and, sometimes, Laurie. My bruised self-esteem longed to hear from my mom, "Great job, Debbie. I'm so proud of you." Or: "You're special and can do whatever you set your mind to, Honey."

Instead, my mother was quick to highlight my flaws. When a pimple appeared on my face like a sunny-side-up egg waiting to be popped, my mother was sure to point it out. A few extra pounds of fat I carried around were examined and judged by Mom's high authority to be an entire cow's worth of fat. Tough crowd.

But with Mr. Benedetto, could it be that perhaps I wasn't as flawed as I thought?

We finally reached my block, and I asked Mr. Benedetto to drop me off nearby. I was only twelve but just felt that, somehow, my mom would question me about my ride, finding a litany of errors, trying to expose some wrongdoing. In my heart, I understood that she was looking out for me on some level, but there was too much criticism involved, and this teacher thought I was fantastic. Groovy. I was ecstatic, and no one was going to kill my buzz.

"Here you go, Debbie. Home now, safe and sound," Mr. Benedetto pronounced. "I'll see you in class tomorrow. Looking forward to our dinner," he added as I scooched out and waved bye.

That night, I was in bed listening to "Ode to Billie Joe" by Bobbie Gentry on my transistor radio. The ride home with Mr. Benedetto circled my mind. Elation surged through me, but confusion was right there waiting for battle. Was having dinner at Mr. Benedetto's okay? Was I that special? I thought I was a bright girl, after all. I got good grades in school. Maybe if I shared Mr. Benedetto's invitation with someone, they could help me make sense of it. Yet, I couldn't. Somewhere, deep inside of me, I knew it wasn't exactly commonplace to go to a teacher's house, even with his wife there. Surely my friends would think I was crazy and wouldn't understand. What would my sisters think? I'm sure they wouldn't approve. They always had a watchful eye over me. As for my mother, I never shared anything with her. My teacher had chosen me, not the other way around, so I decided this would be my secret. It was a surreptitious and enigmatic but amazing dinner invitation that I would keep a secret.

The next day, I lingered around after class with Mr. Benedetto until the other children had left.

"Debbie," he said. "I spoke with my wife, Joy. She can't wait for you to have dinner with us." Placing his hands in both pockets, he continued: "Can you come this Friday evening? If you can wait till after school, you can ride home with me." Each sentence came in a singsong manner, starting in a baritone and ending in soprano. He sounded more like a one-person choir than my history teacher.

"Sure, Mr. Benedetto," I answered, nodding. "I can do that."

"Call me Jim. You can call me Jim when we're not in class. Okay, Debbie?" He was jittery and distracted and kept glancing toward the doorway as if waiting for someone to enter.

The tiny blonde hairs on my arms bristled at that, but I bobbed my head in approval. My teacher was at least twenty years my senior, and it seemed marginally insane for me to call him by his first name. *Whatever*, I thought, and shrugged and went back to calling him Mr. Benedetto.

Friday was just a few days away. I had to figure out how I could explain to my mother why I wouldn't be home after school and where I'd be. Being sneaky became my norm growing up. Fortunately, or unfortunately, I got pretty good at it and rarely got caught. I wasn't yet very terrified of my mom, yet it was hard not to see from the horrors that went on with my siblings what it might look like to get in trouble and the punishment that might take place. There was always so much yelling among them. Tension. Had I been caught in a lie, I knew that it would have been nightmarish. Nevertheless, I put my plan into motion.

"Mommy," I said to get her attention while she was making dinner.

She was mixing the milchig spaghetti in the pot. We consumed this dish often in our home. The word *milchig* is a Yiddish word meaning "made of or derived from milk or dairy products." Since a Jewish dish served without meat was considered milchig, my mother appropriately named the dish milchig spaghetti. It was one of my mother's original creations with the main ingredient, of course, being spaghetti. Added to the spaghetti were a stick of butter, Campbell's tomato soup, and milk. It didn't look nearly as good as it tasted with its unappealing appearance of pasta drenched in bloody-looking milk. As a child, I can still remember how easy the dish was to make and how much fun it was to eat as I slurped up one wiggling pasta strand at a time, the sauce splattering in several directions and making a bloody mess out of my face.

Although milchig spaghetti is not a traditional Jewish dish, it is a dairy dish. Our household did not follow Jewish law when it came to food or other traditions, for that matter. For those who are more religious and follow a kosher diet (meaning food sold, cooked, or eaten by following Jewish law), dairy and meat cannot be eaten together. Not only are they *not* eaten together, but a kosher kitchen must contain a separate set of dishes, cookware, utensils, and even two refrigerators. *Now that's what I'm talking about—two refrigerators mean more food. I can handle that!*

In addition to keeping dairy and meat separate, more stringent laws incorporate procedures in which time must pass when switching from one to the other. For instance, after eating fleischig, the Hebrew word meaning "a dish prepared with or used for meat or meat products," you are supposed to wait a full six hours before eating dairy. I was mortified at the thought of waiting six hours to eat. Could anyone wait that long? If my household practiced Jewish law, fearful of starving before my next meal, I'd strategically eat my last meal right before bedtime. Yep, that way I would surely get in my six hours!

On the other hand, after eating dairy and before eating meat, the customary waiting period is a half hour to an hour. Yeah, I could handle waiting an hour to eat again, but no more. The lesser time between eating dairy and meat (as opposed to meat and dairy) is said to be because dairy does not stick to the palate like meat does. Whenever I thought of this notion, I envisioned a large piece of steak stuck to the top of my mouth for days. I imagined trying to answer a question in school, mouth agape and pointing to the top of my mouth, shouting, "Hey, can't you see? I'm a Jew with a piece of meat stuck up there. Yeah, me, you know, one of the chosen ones—I don't have to participate today because the waiting period is not up until the class is over."

It wasn't until I was much older that I realized that this wasn't at all what sticking to one's palate meant. I still chuckle to myself every time I think of this.

The waiting periods between eating dairy and meat, as well as other Jewish laws, is standard for all Jews who follow the Torah or Hebrew scripture. I was thankful for being brought up in a Reformed Jewish household, the more modern approach to Judaism, whose views are politically progressive, with a propensity toward social justice and one's ability to choose their level of traditional observance. The Conservative Jews, on the other hand, are obligated to follow Jewish law, although there is still a vast range difference of how observance is achieved. Orthodox traditions are more stringent in their beliefs and adhere to a traditional understanding of Jewish law according to rabbinic authorities through the centuries.

Growing up, I was so confused with all this hoopla. At one time, I thought that Jews were the biggest hypocrites that walked the planet. Seriously, I felt that on any given day, you could pick up a menu from the local "How Jewish Do You Want to Be Today?" organization, open the menu, and pick your level of Jewishness. "Today, I'll have a lot of reform topped with a few sprinkles of Conservatism, and for dessert, I'll *try* a bit of Orthodox." I know I am not alone in having wondered over the years if I was a "good Jew" or not. I mean, Judaism is so freaking flexible. If you were like me, you could put on a Jewish costume (not in a literal sense) and appear in temple for a Bar or Bat Mitzvahs or a wedding and still pass for a so-called good Jew.

Moving away from my thoughts of Jewish life, I focused back on my mother and the question I was about to ask. "Mommy." I cleared my throat and raised my voice an octave higher, hoping to get her attention. She was either ignoring me or just couldn't be bothered. Her focus was persistent, like that of a skilled worker. God forbid the blend of that bloody sauce and the pasta wasn't just right. Of course, she rarely stopped what she was doing to focus her attention on me. Being the fifth wheel in the cog of the Barnett household automatically placed my self-worth at the bottom of the hierarchy. *Hey . . . remember me? I'm one of those six kids you forgot you had.* The thought made me grimace in a bellyache sort of way.

"Yes?" she finally answered, pouring the pasta into a large spaghetti dish.

"I was invited to Jill's house to hang out after school on Friday, and she asked me to stay for dinner. Is that okay?" Jill was a friend and neighbor.

"Yes, but make sure you're home by eight at the latest." She peered my way and pointed her finger at me as she continued. "I don't want you up to any funny business, understand? By the way, I will not be working in your father's office tomorrow morning. I was invited to a luncheon at Woodbridge Country Club. We must be there by eleven, which means I have to leave here at ten-thirty."

"Okay, I understand," I said, suddenly losing my appetite at the words "funny business."

My mother's weekdays consisted of working in my dad's dental office from 9:00 A.M. to 12:00 P.M. During that time, she was his bookkeeper and receptionist; however, I think she failed the receptionist course. Although working for my dad saved a salary, I was pretty sure she lost more business for him than not. Shortly after they arrived in the office, my father would get busy working on his first patient. Mom, on the other hand, got busy on the phone, arranging her social schedule for the upcoming days preventing any calls from new patients or current patients wanting an appointment. Plus, call waiting was still a few years away from existence.

Had her time been spent organizing a Girl Scout or PTA meeting—foreign, bizarre concepts to my mother—it might have made more sense, but that was not the case. And the constant gossip. I can still hear the intent and animation in her voice as she rambled, "She did *what*?" and "That boy of hers is no good!" and "That husband of hers cannot be trusted." I knew all this firsthand because I was there helping during summer vacation. On the days I was there, and after she left for her afternoon mah jongg game, I'd clean the lipstick stains she'd leave behind on the phone receiver and shake my head in dismay.

Still, perplexed at the thought of what "funny business" meant, I crossed my heart and swore on my love for Davy Jones. It was apparent from the tone in my mother's voice and her spoken word that she did not trust me. I had not given her a reason to distrust me, or at least not yet. Asking her permission to do anything was not followed by a "yes" or a "no," but rather, "Don't let me catch you doing something I don't approve of" or "I'd better not find out you've been up to no good." Her words of suspicion and doubt only solidified my need to lie again eventually—as I had that day.

Chapter 3

When the last bell rang on Friday, Mr. Benedetto stopped me in the hallway and said, "Debbie, why don't you walk over to the bus stop and wait for me? I'll pick you up. Maybe it's not such a great idea to have other teachers see us leaving together." He offered a wink and a smile, but it didn't relax me.

Why? Are we doing something wrong? I wondered. As I walked to the bus stop, my head whirled with a howling tornado of crazy-ass thoughts. I contemplated backing out but stayed the course.

Shortly after arriving at the bus stop, Mr. Benedetto's car pulled up. As I grabbed the door handle, he reached over the seat and pushed the door open for me. I hurried in, and off we went. The radio was playing "To Sir with Love" by Lulu, which was one of my all-time favorite songs from a film that had come out that summer. I thought,

How funny! Here's a song about a teacher playing at the exact moment I'm in Mr. Benedetto's car. I giggled at that, which made him glance over at me, seemingly tickled, even if he was currently out of the loop.

The ride was long because of the built-up anticipation of meeting my teacher's wife. A weird tension escalated with deafening silence, even with music blaring from the stereo.

"We're here," Mr. Benedetto finally declared, looking like a blissful child who'd just found a hidden Easter egg.

I let myself out of the car. Before we even reached the front door, Mrs. Benedetto appeared almost instantly to greet us. She was lovely. Holy smoke! *Perfection,* I thought. She wore shiny white boots that stopped just below her knees and a minidress covered in brightly colored swirls, pinched tightly at the waist. I wondered how the heck she could breathe. *Maybe she's going to dance on the table for me like one of those go-go girls I saw pictured in my sister's* Seventeen *magazine.*

I couldn't help but notice she had long blonde hair like me, which was pulled back into a ponytail, precisely flipped up at the ends, which perfectly complemented her model figure. Phew . . .

she was the real deal and every bit as pretty as Jeannie from one of my favorite shows, *I Dream of Jeannie.*

She welcomed me with a soft hug and warm touch. I wondered if I should curtsy or something. Then she grabbed me by the hand, motioning me inside, and said, "Hello! You must be Debbie. I'm Mrs. Benedetto, of course. Welcome! Welcome to our home. I'm delighted you could make it. Mr. Benedetto has told me so much about you."

Far out, I thought. *Does she know I'm not a celebrity? This is cool, but I don't know what I did to deserve the red-carpet fanfare.*

"Nice to meet you, Mrs. Benedetto," I replied sheepishly. I was embarrassed and flattered at the same time. I followed awkwardly, hand in hand with Mrs. Benedetto. The sensation of wanting to let go felt as strong as two magnets repelling each other.

What exactly had Mr. Benedetto said about me? Why was I an important enough topic of conversation between my teacher and his wife? I quickly dismissed this thought as we made our way into the house. Mr. Benedetto escorted me to the kitchen table, and we both sat down while Mrs. Benedetto went off to the kitchen to get our dinner.

The table was set magnificently with light-turquoise dishes and a fancy napkin inside every napkin ring. Each one sat diagonally across a plate, positioned on an exquisite ivory-lace tablecloth. A colorful bouquet sat in the middle of the table. I was in awe of how stunning everything looked. I wondered if this was how the table was set each night. In my house, a table procured so ideally would have meant that it had to be either Passover or Thanksgiving.

Mrs. Benedetto made a few trips to the table with delicious food: mashed potatoes drenched in gravy, string beans glistening with droplets of butter, Pillsbury crescent rolls baked to perfection with their golden-brown edges. She served each item to us in a refined manner, from the left side. She joined us for the final dish: a pot roast surrounded by carrots and mushrooms. "Help yourself, dear," Mrs. Benedetto said as she handed the platter to me.

I made a note of how lovely she was, with her little turned-up nose and her glossy hair. She was a statuesque woman, almost to the point of being too thin, yet shapely. Mrs. Benedetto towered over her husband, which reminded me of two of my favorite cartoon characters, Popeye and his girlfriend, Olive Oyl. The thought amused me so much that it made me snicker. Thankfully, though, it was ignored by the Benedettos. I resumed eating, keeping my smirk in check.

We all ate, but I ate way more than usual. I ate so much that they probably thought I wasn't fed at home. "Good," Mrs. Benedetto said with a warm smile. "I'm glad you like it."

"Oh! It's all extremely delicious," I told her, bringing a napkin to my mouth. "You're an excellent cook."

After we'd finished dinner, I helped Mrs. Benedetto clear the table. Then, while we ate her homemade brownies, I covertly did a cursory examination of the room, noticing the all-too-familiar plastic-covered vinyl sofa and chairs. They looked almost exactly like the ones at my home. While I was busy nosily spying their furniture, Mr. Benedetto cleared his throat, ready to speak.

"Debbie, my wife, Joy, and I have what's called an 'open marriage.' Have you ever heard of an open marriage? Do you know what that is?" Mr. Benedetto cleared his throat again, appearing oddly uncomfortable as he shifted around in his seat.

I thought for a moment, tugged at my earlobe, nearly yanking out an earring in the process, and looked around the room for some answers. Maybe it had something to do with the Hare Krishnas? I'd seen them on a few TV shows. Didn't they dress differently? Or perhaps it was listening to jazz and wild types of music? Maybe not. I knew that marriage was between two people. Maybe an open marriage was when the husband and wife talked about things they weren't supposed to? When the answers didn't come, I looked back at Mr. Benedetto. My mind was racing faster than I could think. I could barely focus and had slid partway off the chair. I managed to compose myself when finally I stuttered out the words, "N-No, n-no, Mr. Benedetto. S-Sorry. I don't know what that is."

"Let me explain," he continued, pulling at his shirt collar. Was he finding it difficult to breathe? "An open marriage is when the husband and wife agree that it's okay to be intimate with others. Do you understand? Do you know what being intimate is?" He leaned toward me and placed his hand on my forearm. His touch felt warm yet different and unfamiliar. I pulled back slightly, and he released his grip. I smiled and laughed. I knew this one! It was perfume! "Intimate" by Revlon. I had heard commercials on the radio advertise it and had even seen ads in *Vogue* and *Cosmopolitan*. I always sneaked a peek when my sisters left them lying around. One advertisement said, "What Makes a Shy Girl Get Intimate?" Yet another claimed, "Something Intimate Is Going On."

But Mr. Benedetto had said "being intimate." What did that have to do with perfume? Maybe he meant a douche? When I was nine, I found Annabelle's douches in a box under the sink, took one out, opened it, and brought it to her, asking, "What's this?"

She violently snatched it out of my hand, then calmly told me never to drink it because it was for older girls' intimate parts to stay fresh. I remember thinking to myself that soap worked just fine, and I wasn't about to down something that smelled like that.

Was Mr. Benedetto referring to douching? Did it have something to do with my *intimate parts*? Suddenly, my face flushed beet-red, and I put my hands to my face, hoping to cover my crimson cheeks and forehead.

They smiled at me as I turned the words "being intimate" in my mind and forced myself not to crawl under the table. My head throbbed as my brain tried to catch up with my thoughts. I had bitten my lips raw, and my parched mouth yearned for water.

As I kept thinking about it, I remembered that I had heard the word *intimacy* before. It had been spoken about in hushed tones among my older sisters and even on my favorite soap opera, *General Hospital*. On TV, they kissed and held hands and stuff. Was that the same thing? Was that *intimacy*?

I spoke reticently, letting out a little squeak on the first syllable. "Mr. Benedetto, when you say 'open marriage' and 'being intimate,' are you talking about perfume or intimacy?" I said that last word almost as a whisper, lowering my eyes. Surely, he couldn't mean *that*.

The Benedetto pair chuckled at my question, but I didn't think it was funny, and I certainly wasn't in on the joke. He replied, "I mean intimacy, Debbie. Sex."

That's what it meant on *General Hospital* too! Whoa. This was *not okay*. I thought, *They know I'm only twelve years old, right?* I hadn't realized I'd twisted a chunk of hair around each index finger until my scalp started pulsating and my head began to throb. When I let go, my fingers were left with red-and-white stripes, reminding me of a piece of the fruit-striped gum I had in my purse.

The only things I knew about sex were from my mother. First, it was wrong, wrong, wrong, wrong. I had heard my mom mention sex a few times to my sisters, but it was always in the context of being a very *bad* thing—a *no-no* sort of thing. Second, my mom told me to never, ever sit on a boy's lap because, if I did, I'd get pregnant. And although I remembered seeing a woman on television with a large, protruding belly mention the word *pregnant*, I still wasn't exactly sure what *getting pregnant* meant. Although, *that* was a terrible thing too.

What did Mr. and Mrs. Benedetto want from me? I was more perplexed than ever. *Was Mr. Benedetto inviting me to . . . kiss?*

That settles it! I'm not sitting on his lap! No way! Or, for that matter, Mrs. Benedetto's lap, either! I mean, who knows what could happen? I'm not taking any chances.

I still didn't understand what Mr. Benedetto was getting at, but my gut flipped around enough to tell me it was weird and maybe even perverted or disgusting. How did I wind up in this situation? The words *intimacy*, *sex*, and *pregnancy* swirled around in my brain. I pictured myself in *The Wizard of Oz* scene, when the tornado took Dorothy and her bedroom up, up, and away! Or maybe if I closed my eyes hard and repeated over and over again, "There's no place like home, there's no place like home," I would awake from this bad dream and find myself back in my bedroom, safe from the clutches of the Benedettos.

But I didn't, and Mr. Benedetto leaned in and said, "Mrs. Benedetto and I would love to teach you about intimacy and sex. We'd like to include you in our open marriage."

I held back a scream—no, a cry for help. I was short of breath. I hadn't misunderstood. This teacher, a man I had looked up to, was about to send me straight to purgatory. And since I was Jewish, I wasn't quite sure if that was worse than going down to that fiery pit with Satan or just never going to heaven at all. Or was I stuck in the middle—somewhere between heaven and hell—while being punished? Damn them. I didn't want to know.

Suddenly I heard Azzie Mae's words to me: "Child, if it smells like rotten eggs and it ain't coming from the trash, run. Run like hell."

Good plan. Thanks, Azzie.

Fear and shame squeezed the last breath out of me, and the voice inside my head screamed, *Get out of there—quick!* I was so good at lying and sneaking behind my mother's back that I was confident I could quickly find a way to get out of this one. I asked to use the bathroom, pretending as if I'd never heard what he'd just told me. Hesitantly, I walked backward, mostly, until I knew that I wouldn't fall—or be dragged—into Mr. or Mrs. Benedetto's lap. There was no way I was getting pregnant—whatever that meant—even by accident.

I must've looked odd walking backward, because they both cocked their heads, staring at me as if I were a stranger knocking on their door, asking for a cup of sugar. I thought it was funny that when both their eyebrows went up, and their heads went to the side, they almost looked like Lassie when she was puzzled. I reached the little girls' room without incident, thankfully, and sat on the toilet while my mind went to work, thinking of every kind of excuse to leave. When I finally figured out my exit strategy, I returned to the table.

"Mr. and Mrs. Benedetto, thank you so much for dinner. You're . . . um . . . very generous. It was delicious. But it's getting late. I promised to be home by seven P.M. to keep my younger brother company while my parents go out." *How'd I done?* I wondered while my body trembled as if experiencing a magnitude ten earthquake.

Mr. Benedetto stood up rather abruptly with his mouth opened wide enough that I could see his silver fillings. Mrs. Benedetto's eyes widened, and her back stiffened against her chair. I sucked in my breath, waiting for something to be said. Maybe if I held it long enough, I would die, and this could all be over.

"Shall we go?" he said. The pleasantness of his voice indicated he could sense my resistance and horror over the proposition.

Oh, man. Yes! Please, let's go. An intense feeling of relief flooded over me. A humongous wave had swallowed me as if an angel had shielded me with her glorious wings of protection. I was free! I could make my escape without perfume, douches, sitting on laps, or sex—because that was a no-no—and any other weird stuff my once-favorite teacher was implying.

The ride home was about as awkward as it could get. I barely took in a breath of air, not wanting to disturb the silence that permeated through the car. I peered out the window to avoid even a glimpse of Mr. Benedetto. At one point, I heard him clear his throat and wished he'd choke on his words, those words, *open marriage* and *intimacy*.

For the rest of the school year, I avoided any private conversations with Mr. Benedetto. I made no eye contact with him and became physically ill before entering his class each day. Nevertheless, I attended class and did my assignments just the same. I was utterly thankful that he never approached me again about that evening. Maybe he had realized my reaction had been enough of a sign that I was not a willing participant of whatever he was offering. The burden had been lifted, in any case. I never told a soul. And I was grateful that after the incident with the bullying, I would be attending a new school for my eighth-grade year.

Chapter 4

In 1968, I lied to my mother again—one of many ways I learned to weave a lie just for her; only this time, my lie met the devil himself face-to-face.

I had left a note in my pocket that my best girlfriend, Donna, passed me in class. My mother found it and approached me, ferociously waving the note in the air like a paper airplane spinning out of control, the inflection in her voice rising with each word she screamed.

"Who wrote you this note?"

"My best friend, Donna Stone," I answered, trembling. Anticipating a slap, I stepped back, raised my hands, and crossed them at the wrist to guard my face.

"I cannot believe she used the word *shit*!" Spit flew out of my mother's mouth as she yelled.

"Any girl who uses bad words like that is no good. You are forbidden from spending time with her outside of school. Do you hear me?" The wet sprays of saliva hit me, adding insult to her words.

"Yes," I said as tears welled up in my eyes. At that moment, I hated my mother more than anything. As I walked away, my head nearly touching the ground, all I could think was, *There is no way I am not going to spend time with my very best friend. Who does my mother think she is?*

Donna and I met at New Haven Hebrew Day School, the religious school where my parents sent me after my traumatic experience with the bullies at Sheridan. There was an instant connection between us, and we soon became besties. We had so much fun together and were alike in so many ways. Both of us were twelve years old and boy crazy, so it was not surprising that boys were the topic of most conversations: who we thought was cute, what base we would dare to go if we had a boyfriend, and so on. She had the same kind of free-spirited personality I did. Whenever Donna and I would leave each other, we'd embrace tightly until we finally let go and gasped for air, as if coming up from water. We'd follow it up with a loud cackle.

The next morning after my altercation with my mother, I walked to the bus stop thinking about how much I loved being with Donna. I couldn't imagine my life without her. We picked each other to be besties, and there was nothing I wouldn't do to keep her in my life. I hopped on the bus, which was already waiting for me. On the ride to school, I leaned against the window and gazed out at the houses and trees passing me by. I smiled at the thought of seeing Donna until my smile was usurped by a mother pulling a little girl abruptly by the hand, nearly causing her to fall over. *That poor kid. Why is she so rough with her? But, at least . . .* And then my thoughts flashed back to my mother, who as far back as I could remember, never held my hand while we walked together. At least this mother cared enough to hold her child's hand and be with her. And then my mother's words careened right back into my head: "Any girl who uses bad words like that is no good." The words reverberated over and over, until they were raveled inside me like one of the tightly wound balls of yarn I used for knitting. I dropped my head into my hands and thought, *How am I going to pull off seeing my best friend without my mother finding out?*

I had concocted a lie about having to stay after school that day to make up some work so I could hang with Donna. We met after the last class and meandered to her bus, which dropped us off near her house. I was always jazzed to visit her home. Her mom was such a cool and hip lady, and no comparison to my mother who was just the opposite.

We hung in her room playing pickup sticks and watching *General Hospital*, *Dark Shadows*, and then *The Dating Game* on her fifteen-inch black-and-white TV set handed down to her by her parents when they got their first colored set. Once we finished all three shows, it was time to leave.

I looked at Donna with a pout and muttered, "I hate it when I have to leave you."

"Me too," Donna replied in a low, sullen voice.

She walked me to the bus stop, and on the way, I finally got the guts to tell her about the incident with my mother. I was worried she might let it come between our friendship. "Hey, I have to tell you what happened between my mother and me the other day. But you have to promise me you won't let this come between our friendship."

"Seriously, what could ruin our friendship?"

I walked in front of Donna on the sidewalk and stopped abruptly. I placed a hand on each of her shoulders, looked her square in the eyes, and said, "I am serious. This is bad—I mean, *bad*! I am even embarrassed to share it with you, but you must know because I cannot see you unless I lie to my mother."

"Okay, now you've got me worried. Just tell me already." Donna moved my hands off her shoulders and put her hands on her hips, as if waiting for a bomb to drop.

"Remember the note you passed me in class the other day?"

"Yeah, what about it?"

"My mom found it in my pocket and read it."

"Okay, I mean, I'd be pretty upset if my mom read my stuff too, but it's not the end of the world, right?"

"You used the word *shit* in the note. She thinks you are going to be a bad influence on me, which is so absurd."

"Oh, God, it's all my fault. I must be more careful. I didn't mean to get you in trouble. My mom doesn't like me using those words, either." Donna started to cry.

"Don't cry. Please don't cry. It'll be a little harder to see each other, but we can and we will." I grabbed her hand. We walked hand in hand until we reached the bus stop. We embraced with our usual goodbye hug, only this time we squeezed each other a bit harder.

I boarded the bus, sat down, and noticed the lingering tightness around my rib cage. I rested my head against the seat and thought again about how lucky I was to have Donna as my best friend. I had successfully pulled off my first big lie to my mother and shared what happened with Donna. I closed my eyes and daydreamed about how awesome it would be to appear as a contestant on *The Dating Game*.

When the bus arrived at the corner of Lakeview Terrace and Fountain Street, I was still on a high from my afternoon with Donna. When I exited the bus, instead of walking down each step, I leaped over two and flung forward, landing on both hands. *Damn, that was pretty dumb.* My hands were burning. I got up and brushed off the fragments of pebbles and noticed they both looked like the aftereffects of horrendous acne I'd seen on some boys, red and craterlike.

The bus finished letting everyone off. No one noticed I had fallen, or maybe they did, and strangers weren't supposed to offer help. The bus took off and left a plume of exhaust that lingered in the air. I let out a gagging cough and spotted a familiar car parked on the other side of the street. I swallowed with a hard gulp. My saliva was stuck in my throat as if it had submerged into a large cotton field. *Shit! Drat!* I thought . . . *I'm in trouble. You are a lame duck now. My mother must have found out somehow. She never picks me up at the bus stop.*

There was a demeanor that followed my mother around, the kind that let you know you should be frightened of her—and I was. What I couldn't figure out was how in the world she found out that I had spent the afternoon with Donna. I was screwed, caught in a big, whopping, motherfucking lie!

Again.

As I crossed the street, the earth moved under me as if I were being transported by one of those moving walkways in an airport, pushing me slowly toward fate and my mother's car. The heat of the day seared the thoughts swirling around my head. I pleaded to God that I was wrong in my suspicions of what lay ahead. The dampness under my armpits grew into large circles of sweat, causing the fabric to stick to my skin.

I approached the car. I looked up at the sky, inhaled a deep breath, and just before getting in, I muttered, *God, help me.* Within seconds, she started wailing: "How dare you disobey me! You went behind my back and got together with *that slut* of a friend." Her face was gnarled, and she resembled the Wicked Witch of the West. She lunged at me after spitting out all the accusatory words possible. My eyes widened to match my gaping mouth, and I threw up my arms, crossed at the wrists, to protect my face while backing up as close to my door as possible.

I was hoping to stave her off with my screams. "Stop! Stop!" But she continued her jabs. She could have been an Ali contender. Finally, she pulled away, put the car in drive, and sped toward our house, leaving a trail of burning rubber behind that had seeped in through the exhaust.

She continued with what sounded like a jail sentence. "Don't you ever let me find out that you're seeing *that* girl again. You don't want to know what's in store for you if there is ever a next time. Even though you told me you had to stay after school, I had a feeling you were up to no good, so I called the school and found out you weren't there. Then I called your friend Tina, and she told me you were meeting *that girl* after school."

I was still in shock by what had just happened. We drove home in deafening silence. I couldn't shed a tear because the anger had dried up every ounce of emotion I felt. When we got home, I declined dinner and went directly to my room. I was defeated and humiliated under her power and powerless in my world of Donna and Debbie, which had just blown up into smithereens. I lay in bed fully clothed, my mother's words clattering in my thoughts: *That girl . . . that slut.* I was sick to my stomach, my heart broken into a trillion pieces. The last thing that went through my head before I fell asleep was, *How could one bad word like* shit *turn someone into a slut without a name?*

The next morning, I decided to call my sister Laurie about the Donna lie. Since I was so downtrodden by the whole situation, I thought she might console me and defend my position. She usually did when it came to Mother, or at least lovingly listened to me.

"Laur?" I tearfully said through the receiver.

"Hey, Deb, what's up?"

I proceeded to tell her what had happened. All the anger I had felt toward my mother the day before came gushing out of me in monsoon proportion.

"Try to get a hold of yourself, Deb. You know how Mommy is. Anything she can make into a negative, she does. Nonetheless, you really shouldn't have lied, although I understand why you did. I'm so sorry you had to go through that. It isn't fair that you are forbidden from seeing your best friend."

Still sobbing but calming down a bit, I wiped the snot that had already made its way into my mouth onto my pajama top and said, "I know, I know. I just can't believe I can never see Donna again . . . well, except during school, that is."

"You'll make new friends, Deb. Maybe this is best, even though you might not understand this now."

"Thanks for listening. I love you, Laur."

"Love you too. On another note, can you babysit this Saturday night?"

"Sure." My tears were drying. "What time will you pick me up?"

"Five thirty if that works for you."

"Yeah, sure."

"See ya then. Love ya."

After hanging up with Laurie, I halfheartedly got dressed and recounted the previous day's events. My heart filled with thoughts of Donna and our times together while my eyes welled again. I was losing her. I dreaded seeing her at school because I'd have to break the news to her.

My mother's reaction festered inside me like a terminal disease. Her aloof way of parenting was like a bad mystery that would never be solved. And her behavior on that day was indicative of her absenteeism. Although her social life was vital to her and possibly more important than her kids, she felt an obligation to keep an eye on us and to stave off the guilt she felt for not being home—a lot. Throughout my childhood, she held a watchful eye on my older brother Gary, myself, and my younger brother Kenny by calling our friends to see if we were where we said. I was never caught in another lie because my mother put the fear of God in me that day. Of course, I did lie again, but I didn't get caught. I learned to cover my tracks. And just as Laurie had said, I made a new best friend. Her name was Anat Abrams. She was the new girl at Hebrew Day School who moved to the States from Israel. She spoke very little English and was extremely shy. I tended to befriend the underdog, making friends with the fat girl in the neighborhood everyone made fun of, or the homely, unpopular girl. I was neither fat (although my mother would affirm differently) nor homely, and I was not popular, either. The popular girls, from what I surmised, had similarities; they had mothers who greeted them at the door when they returned from school, wore expensive clothes, and had beautifully dressed rooms in frilly pink and purple flowers and lace.

But not me.

I remember the first day I introduced myself to Anat on the bus ride home.

I licked my lips until they felt irritated, and then I mustered up the guts to approach her.

"Hi, my name is Debbie. You must be the new girl. What's your name?"

"I'm Anat, and I don't speak perfect English." Her eyes peered away from me. She tugged at her uniform skirt, as if wanting to pull it off.

"Where are you from, Anat?"

"Israel. My abba and ima moved here to go into business with a relative."

I stood tall and thrust out my chest. I was proud I knew those words meant "mother" and "father" in Hebrew.

"Mind if I sit next to you?" Without waiting for her to answer, I pulled my backpack off in preparation.

"Sure."

I settled in next to her, our arms touching a tad, so she moved over. We started chatting, and I noticed her English was far better than she let on. Slowly, she eased up and leaned into me. Her long, brown wavy hair was half tied up by a large ribbon that spanned bigger than the width of her head. The rest fell just above her waist. I couldn't help noticing how her eye color perfectly matched her hair. We got to know each other on that bus ride. She was soft-spoken and sweet.

We were approaching her bus stop, which came before mine. I whispered, "I guess this is where you get off." I stood up and moved to the aisle to let her out.

"Yeah," she said. In her voice, I could detect that she didn't want the bus ride to end, either.

"Hey." My tone perked up. "Maybe this weekend we can hang out or something. Maybe even see a movie. *Planet of the Apes* just came out, and I cannot wait to see it."

"I'll ask my mother and let you know tomorrow at school."

"Out of sight," I blurted out.

"Huh . . . what does this 'out of sight' mean?"

I realized she was just getting familiar with our language, let alone understanding our slang. "I'm sorry. 'Out of sight' is slang for 'great' or 'wonderful.' But don't worry, I'll teach you all our slang words and expressions. Promise."

"Ahhh, we have very similar slang in Hebrew too." Anat got off the bus, and as the bus pulled away, we waved to each other.

That weekend, Anat and I went to see *Planet of the Apes*. It took no time at all for us to become best friends. We often hung out at her house. My mother approved of Anat because she didn't swear, not even one tiny bit. I was wondering if Anat was as "pure as the driven snow." I had heard my mother say that once in a conversation with my sister Joanne. What my mother didn't know is that Anat didn't swear because she was still navigating our language and swear words were not yet a part of her vocabulary. *Phew!* I thought. *I won't have to worry about her writing me a note as Donna did.*

Anat was not interested in boys, and I found that very strange. I think her shy tendencies and language barrier kept her from even considering the thought. Boys were pretty much all I had on my mind. Anat, the good friend that she was, listened to my constant chatter about cute boys, although she wasn't consumed with the opposite sex as I was.

Hebrew Day School sat right in the middle of an Italian neighborhood, and many of the Italian boys would hang out just outside the fence surrounding the school courtyard. I had my eye on one adorable boy named Bobby, and he had his eye on me. We flirted through the chain-link fence and eventually started a conversation. He reminded me of John Lennon with perfectly coiffed hair that converged with his bushy eyebrows, and his hair color paired splendidly with his chestnut-shaped eyes. He had me hook, line, and sinker pretty much from our first glance.

One day after school, Bobby approached me while I was waiting to board the school bus.

"Hey, blondie. Why don't you hang with us instead of going home right away?" He was referring to the group of guys he hung out with regularly. "You can always take the city bus home."

He grabbed the cigarette from behind his ear and lit it up. The smoke fumes pleasantly greeted my nostrils. There was something about the smell of freshly lit cigarettes that appealed to me.

"Uh . . . uh . . ." I stammered. I gazed at Anat, who was standing next to me, squinting her eye. She shook her head in disapproval.

"Hang on," I said to Bobby.

I tugged at Anat's arm and motioned for her to follow me. When we were far away enough from Bobby, my shoulders slumped, and I placed my hands on my hips. "What's wrong? It'll be okay. Nothing wrong with me hanging out with them for a bit. You can stay too, ya know."

She lowered her head. I could see she was disappointed that I would not be accompanying her on the ride home.

"Ahhh . . . go ahead, then," Anat said sullenly. "I just . . . well, I look forward to our ride home together. I can't stay. My mother is strict about monitoring my homework sessions."

Hmmm . . . Do mothers monitor homework sessions? It sounds like an oxymoron to me. I'd be lucky if my mother observed any part of my life.

I placed both hands on her shoulders and said, "Tomorrow, I promise tomorrow."

After the school bus left, Bobby, his friends, and I walked over to his house just a block away and hung out on his front stoop. We smoked cigarettes, something I had already been doing for more than two years, while the boys smoked a joint. I had not yet started smoking pot, so I declined when they offered. I knew my older brother smoked the stuff, but I wasn't daring enough to try it—yet. Smoking cigarettes, on the other hand, was considered cool, and everyone wanted to be cool.

I had also heard that smoking marijuana could cause acne, blindness, or even sterility. I was not about to take my chances until I knew the facts. Especially when it came to the sterility thing. Someday I wanted kids, and the thought of doing anything to prevent that scared the bejesus out of me. I had also heard of stuff called LSD. A kid in school said it caused hallucinations. *Maybe I should have used some before that fateful day with Donna. My mind could have tricked me into seeing Glinda, the Good Witch of the South, in the car instead of the Wicked Witch of the West.* I let out a cackle.

"What's so funny?" Bobby said, followed by an even louder cackle of his own from being stoned.

"Oh, nothing. I just had some funny thoughts in my head—nothing to do with you."

I saw the other three boys huddled together, talking among themselves. They all grabbed their bikes, hopped on, and one after the other cried out, "We gotta split, Bobby."

Bobby and I stayed seated on the stoop. He slid his hand over mine, and when he didn't sense resistance, he intertwined each finger with mine. Tingly shockwaves coursed through my entire body. It was the first time I had held hands with a boy since walking home with my fourth-grade boyfriend.

I continued to hang out with Bobby just once a week because I didn't want to upset Anat. To me, her friendship was as vast as an ocean. Over time, Bobby and I grew closer, and I even allowed him to kiss me on the lips. My very first kiss on the lips. It was nice. It made my insides ignite like a fire spreading from the very top of my head down to my toes. I tried to picture my mother and father embracing or kissing because up until this point, my mother had made it clear that there should be separation between boys and girls. Shortly after I started menstruating, I remember her saying, "Don't ever sit on a boy's lap because if you do, you will get pregnant." Of course, I tried to find this information in the Britannica encyclopedia, but with no success, I let it go. I never knew what all the fuss was about on *General Hospital* and why the actors were kissing in every other scene. Now I knew. And to think, a year ago, I didn't understand the difference between Intimate cologne and being intimate with someone.

The last day of school neared, and the anticipated summer months rang in my ears like the Freedom Bell we had so graciously gifted to the Germans in 1950. Summer. Freedom. Fun. New adventures. They were all synonymous with my almost thirteen-year-old mind. I was about to become an official teenager on July 17. That meant I had two years left to get my driver's permit, and five to become legal so I could live on my own. My life couldn't pass by quick enough, and certainly not as quickly as the changing times.

Lyndon B. Johnson had completed his term in office after initially taking the presidential seat upon the death of President John F. Kennedy.

Some adored him and others despised him. I was on the adoring side; after all, he signed the bill for the Civil Rights Act of 1964 that banned racial discrimination in public facilities. Although this was one big step for the Black man, they were far from being equal to the white man. Azzie was never far from my thoughts when I recalled her struggles.

Richard Nixon had become our thirty-seventh president. In a few months, we'd be welcoming in the seventies, yet the counterculture and its antiestablishment movement of the sixties had not slowed down, and young men were still being drafted into the war.

School was out and summer was upon us. The first party of summer was in full swing, and I was feeling no pain both literally and figuratively. The hurt from the loss of Donna's friendship and the day my mother turned into the Wicked Witch of the West were both fading into the thick marijuana smoke that lingered in the room like an obscure blanket of fog. I spotted my brother's friend James through the parting fumes. He was quite the hunk, with a head of soft curls. I spied him carefully like an animal ready to dig its claws into a piece of meat until he finally noticed me.

Our eyes locked together.

Chapter 5

News spread fast in our neighborhood, but not as quickly as the marijuana fumes at Patricia's party. Patricia, who lived in a neighborhood close by, was throwing a party on a Saturday night. Her parents were going on a weekend getaway, and her oldest brother was watching over Patricia and her younger sister. Without social media in 1968, we used one landline after another to spread the news of a big party. Before long, the entire neighborhood knew about Patricia's house party.

The marijuana smoke cast a thick layer of low-hanging clouds in Patricia's kitchen, making it nearly impossible to see faces until I parted the smoke with my hands. The music was blasting, some of the girls were dancing, and several boys had a glass of beer in one hand or swigging right out of the bottle. Before I knew it, a person on my left passed me a joint. After I took a hit, he motioned to me to pass it on to the person on my right. The joint continued to pass me on the way back and forth to the person on my left and right. I was the pot smoker's middleman—getting twice the hits and doubly stoned.

"Deb, come join us."

Patricia and another friend motioned for me to join them as they danced to the Creedence Clearwater Revival's "Suzie Q." My head was in the clouds as I bopped my way into the family room just off the kitchen. I joined in, moving and grooving to the music. I spotted my brother's friend, James. He had the cutest butt ever. He appeared to be just under six feet tall. We made eye contact a few times.

"He's looking at you," Patricia mouthed as she tilted her head in James's direction.

"I know," I mouthed back.

"Well, then, why don't you go over and talk to him?"

Without saying anything else, I made my way over to James.

"Hi! You're my brother Gary's friend, right?"

"Yes, I'm James. You're Debbie, I'm guessing?"

I swayed my body toward him, nudging him slightly, hoping he'd dance with me, but I could tell he was not at all interested in making himself look like a fool.

"Awww, come on," I said, tugging playfully at his sleeve.

"Nope, you won't get me to dance." An adorable half-crooked smile met my eyes. I suddenly became flushed while looking into his beautiful blue-green eyes. My body's temperature must have risen from 98.6 to well over 100. Had I been a block of ice, I would have melted right there in front of him. *I'm melting, I'm melting . . .*

When I finally stopped dancing, I decided to get a bit more serious. Being the affectionate girl I was, I placed my hand on his arm and brushed up a little closer to him.

"Hey," he said. "Wanna find a quiet place to talk?"

"Sure, let's check the house out."

He grabbed my hand and pulled me with urgency, darting in and out of packs of kids and almost spilling the entire drink he had in his other hand. We made our way to a long hallway and found a bedroom with an enormous bed, a distinct difference from my parents' twin beds, if indeed this was her parents' bedroom. I was confused; I thought all mothers and fathers slept in separate beds. Even Lucy and Desi Arnaz slept in separate beds. I walked over to the bed and slid my hand along the brocade golden-orange bedspread fringed along the bottom. It felt elegant under my touch. Atop the bed was a large, solid gold-fringed pillow carefully placed in the center.

"This must be her parents' room. I'm not sure it's a good idea to be in here," I said with hesitation in my voice. "You should see my parents' bedroom. This room is a palace in comparison to my parents' room with the two twin beds layered in mismatched cotton blankets."

"Ahhh, come on. We can lock the door. No one will know."

"Okay, but let's be sure of one thing, James: talking only—no fancy stuff, understand?" My mouth became parched, and my mind raced through the possibilities of what might happen next. I suddenly doubted my position here.

"Sure, no problem. I promise. Let's just lie down here so we can talk and get to know each other."

He took a joint out of his pocket and lit it up. We sat on the edge of the bed until we'd smoked most of it. After each hit, he flicked the ashes into his cup. When it was too close to the end to handle, he put it out on the inside of the cup and pocketed the roach—I'm sure for future use. The high eased any doubt I had. And soon I was melting into the mattress and right into James's arms. There was no getting to know each other—well, at least not with words. He started kissing me in a way I had never kissed a boy before. Our tongues were twisting and twirling inside each other's mouths. I was confident we were about to get tongue-tied (pardon the pun).

The more our bodies rolled around on the bed, the higher I felt. I was lost in the rapture of this new and exciting feeling when I felt James reach under the back of my shirt to skillfully and meticulously undo my bra with one hand. *What a pro. Hopefully, this is not one of his regular jobs.* He continued by sliding the straps one at a time down each arm until the bra was freed from the spell I was under. I decided to help, so I grabbed the bra from under my shirt and flung it on the floor.

He lifted my shirt and cupped a breast in his hand.

"They are beautiful," he said.

Beautiful . . . Hmmm I never thought of a breast as being beautiful. Especially not mine.

He started to kiss my breasts, and I could feel my nipple harden under his tongue. The feeling in my groin was new and inviting. I could feel the wetness on my underwear. He pulled his shirt over his head and returned to kissing my breasts. He placed my hand over his pants zipper, instructing me to squeeze his penis. *How awkward. Is it that obvious I have no idea what I am doing?* I wondered. While still kissing me, he arched his body over mine and unsnapped and unzipped my jeans, sliding them down low enough for me to wiggle them off and kick them from the bed.

Before long, we were both naked in Patricia's house on her parents' bed.

"Let's pull the spread off the bed so we don't ruin it," I said.

James helped me, and as he lay back down, I noticed his erection; it was difficult not to see it standing at attention, larger than life with a slight bend to one side. I had never seen one in person. The closest to a real penis I had seen was while bathing with my younger brother when we were very young, or the occasional glimpse at the bulge through my older brother's underwear.

I knew what was going to happen next. After all, girls talk about this sort of thing. It's as if we prepare ourselves before the big day even comes. "Sure, no problem, Debbie" were empty words, but I didn't seem to mind. Before I knew it, James was back on top of me, kissing me passionately.

"James," I whispered in his ear, "this is my first time—I'm a virgin. Is this going to hurt?"

"Don't worry. I'll take it slow. I will be careful and make sure you're okay."

There was something kind and caring about James. His words soothed me, and I trusted him. He reached his hands between my legs and slowly inserted one finger, then two. I was able to handle one on my own, but two I had never experienced. Even though it hurt a little, the pleasure overwhelmed me.

He groaned in a low hum, which sounded more like a diesel engine idling nearby. James positioned himself on top of me and slowly inserted his penis. With each push, he'd stop to make sure I was okay. It did hurt, but I lied and said I was okay. Once he was inside me, I was so thankful the pain disappeared. No more than two minutes later, his hum turned into a wail. It scared the crap out of me, and when he collapsed on top of my body, I thought, *He might be having a heart attack.* Then with a sigh of relief, I heard him say, "That was nice." The sweat ran down his face and onto his chest. Our bodies slithered around in a pool of wetness, and it felt gross to me. So gross that all I could think of was getting home and showering.

From conversations with other girls about sex and losing one's virginity, I knew that James had had an orgasm, and I knew that I had not. I wasn't surprised; after all, even on my best day alone in my room, the marathon took at least twenty minutes. I chuckled to myself, wondering if any guy could wait that long. We stayed there holding each other for a while. James said it was fantastic and asked me if it was okay for me, wanting to know if I came. I nodded in affirmation; though, I had not, but what I wanted to say was, "You were too busy at work to know."

Once we got up, we made the bed as neatly as we could, hoping we left no secrets behind. I was thankful I didn't ruin the sheets with blood; from what my friends told me, you always bleed when you break your hymen. And then I remembered the day I fell on the bar of my brother's bike, and it all made sense to me. Although I had not lost my virginity that day, I had broken my hymen. Certainly now, the pain I had experienced on that day made so much more sense to me. As we walked back to the party, I recalled that fateful day.

~ ~ ~

Gary's bike was too small for him, so he offered it to me. "Hey, Deb," my older brother yelled to me one day after school. "I'm going to use Annabelle's old bike since she's using Laurie's now. Take mine."

"Wow, thanks, Gare!" I grabbed the handles. I noticed the bike was almost as tall as I was. I placed a finger on my upper lip and squinted. What was that strange out-of-place bar connecting from the front of the bike to under the seat? I put one foot on the pedal, but it slipped off. The pedal spun around and around. Waiting for it to stop, I blurted out, "Can I try it now?"

"You sure can, but be careful. It might still be too big for you, and it's a boy's bike, besides."

I climbed on after a few failed attempts. Because the bike was too big for me, I had to straddle myself over the bar. The bike felt awkward under me and challenging to control. The front wheel veered to the left and then to the right, repeatedly. My heart quickened. I was both excited and nervous at the same time. I tried again to keep the front wheel straight but had no success, and then—I hit a bump. I lost complete control, and my body jumped into the air a foot before I went down—smack on the bar.

"Owww!" I shrilled.

"Deb, are you all right?" Gary came racing toward me.

Without answering my brother, I dropped the bike, ran into my house, and bolted to the bathroom. My vagina throbbed with intense pain. It was as if I split myself apart. I lifted my skirt and pulled down my underwear. I began to cry when I saw blood all over my panties. I was lightheaded and gasped for air in between breaths. I let out a wail that reverberated in my head. *Ouch!*

Azzie heard me and came into the bathroom to check things out. "Are you okay?" She took my face into her hands. Shaking her head in dismay, she continued, "Baby Girl, what happened?"

"Gary gave me his bike, so I tried it, but it was too big for me, and I fell onto that big bar."

"Let me take a look." Her calm voice was always there and ready to soothe me.

I lifted my skirt again, and Azzie examined me. "Hold still. How do you expect me to see what's going on if you don't stop moving around?"

"I can't help it," I said through my wails. "As hard as I tried, I couldn't stop jerking around.

After examining me, Azzie confirmed, "You have a little cut on your privates. It might hurt for a while, but I'm pretty sure you will be all right."

"Please don't tell Mommy!"

"Why?"

"Because I just don't want her to know." I stomped my feet, which caused my vagina to hurt even more.

"Alrighty, Baby Girl, but I'm not sure I understand why you won't tell her." She grabbed a tissue and wiped the snot from my face.

"Please, Azzie, don't tell her. I know she'll blame this all on me." I buried my head in my hands. I knew that Azzie had accepted my final plea not to tell my mother; after all, what mattered most to her was my protection.

~ ~ ~

I was thankful in a strange sort of way that all the blood and pain were left behind with that day instead of on Patricia's parents' sheets.

James and I joined the party. No one missed us. Someone handed me a beer, and I brought it to my lips. James pulled my waist toward him and planted a kiss on me.

After that night, James and I saw each other a lot during the summer. We had plenty of sex and smoked a lot of pot, and he even taught me some new things in the bedroom. I knew he would be off to college that fall, and strangely enough, I was just fine with it. That summer fling with James reminded me of the love story between Troy Donahue and Sandra Dee in A Summer Place. That summer in New Haven, Connecticut, we had made our own movie.

I knew there would always be a place for James in my heart, the boy with whom I lost my virginity. He was such a stand-up sort of guy—kind, caring, and thoughtful. But he was off to college, and I was ready to hit the big leagues by entering Richard C. Lee High School just a few weeks ahead. A new school and new boys were on the horizon.

Chapter 6

I'll never forget the day I met Ivan. It was love at first sight—my first true love, for that matter. Ivan was a Ukrainian boy with a full head of long, thick dark hair that fell well below his shoulders and had latched onto my heart like a vine. His bushy eyebrows seemed to match his full lips so perfectly. We first saw each other walking the halls of Richard C. Lee High School, the social ground that connected us with anyone who wasn't in one of our classrooms. Our eyes locked each time we passed each other, and my heart quickened every time he flashed that adorable smile at me. Later that same day, while opening my locker, I felt a tap on my back. I turned to find Ivan a bit too close for comfort, and at that moment, time froze.

"Hi," he said. "Not sure if you know me. I'm Ivan Chovnik."

"I don't." The words purred out of me. "But I've seen you walking in the hallways." I wanted to die right then and there. I fumbled with my books and barely made eye contact with him. Then, like an idiot, the heat on my cheeks rising by the second, I dropped one of my books.

"Hey, let me get that for you." As he bent down, I breathed in what I thought might have been Alberto VO5 shampoo. I closed my eyes and let the scent linger in my nostrils.

He handed the book to me, and with the most darling smile, he uttered nervously, "Would you wanna hang out some time?"

"Yeah, sure," I said with a giddy lilt to my voice.

"Do you think I could have your number?" Now I wasn't the only one blushing.

Fumbling to tear out a page from my notebook, I dropped another book. I swooped down to get it and then jotted down my number and handed him the piece of paper. "Do me a favor," I said, my voice demure. "If anyone but me answers the phone, hang up. My mom will never approve of us. I can tell by your last name you are not Jewish, and my mother will never allow me to hang with a non-Jewish boy." *Did I really say that? He's going to think I'm a whack job now.*

"Gotcha covered. I'll call you later on." He walked away, looking back over his shoulder and giving me the cutest dimpled smile ever.

My thoughts were so absorbed in Ivan and his phone call that I could hardly contain myself. I wished the school day away so I could get home. When the day finally ended with the three o'clock bell, I left school and headed for the bus stop at a marathon pace. Once on the bus, I encountered the longest ride home ever and realized how funny it was that the thought of a phone call could cause a bus ride home to seem endless, but it did.

Later that evening, I lay in bed, the same bed that once belonged to Annabelle. The bed she'd let me share with her when I was a small child but only after bribing me to tickle the underneath part of her arm. I remembered the feeling of excitement and anticipation when she said yes. Now, as I lay in the same bed, *my* bed, with a whole other form of excitement and anticipation, I didn't dare put the transistor on, in fear of missing the phone ring.

After what seemed like hours, the phone rang. I grabbed for the handset and nearly fell off the bed. I picked it up and was disappointed to hear it was someone calling for Gary. I lay back down, worried he'd stay on the phone for too long. If

Ivan called and kept getting a busy signal, he might give up.

I got off the bed and paced a few times, then got back on the bed. The phone rang again. This time, I picked it up so fast that the twisted and coiled handset cord resisted, sending the base of the princess phone spinning out of control.

With the phone dangling in the air, I said, "Hello?" My heart was coming out of my chest. It was Ivan.

I heard someone else lift the receiver, then my mother's voice: "Who is it, Debbie?"

"Just a classmate," I said quickly hoping she had not heard a male voice on the other end.

"Don't tie the line up for long and besides, I am waiting on a few important calls."

I didn't listen. I rarely listened to her. Ivan and I talked for hours. We talked about everything and anything: school, music, the future. We spoke on the phone again over the weekend. The conversation flowed naturally, like a river's journey to its destination, neither of us wanting it to end.

I could hardly wait to see Ivan on Monday, and when Monday came, I was lucky not to stumble over the other kids in the hallway because my eyes were looking out for Ivan and not where I was walking. I was fourteen and had fallen in love, or at least that's what I thought it was. So many new and exciting things were happening to me and around me. I was thrilled to have transitioned from private school into the public high school system. Being able to wear skirts above the knee was far out. At Hebrew Day, getting caught wearing your skirt even a millimeter above your knee was like Eve getting caught eating the forbidden fruit. We did it anyway, or at least until we got caught.

I was enthralled with the vast differences between the private and public school sectors, which already had its distinct contrasts. Still, after 1967, more lenient dress code policies in the public schools made those differences even more extreme. Miniskirts and knee-high boots for the girls, long hair, and more distinct sideburns for the boys along with bell-bottom jeans were the craze. We could wear current styles in public schools. I, for one, adored wearing my miniskirts, knee-high boots, or bell-bottom jeans—all doing justice to them in my lanky five-foot-seven frame. It was a time when "thin was in." I certainly fit the bill and was chosen to be the school yearbook model for my graduating class of '73. I even did some modeling during high school, but it was short-lived. I was so intimidated by the other thin, pretty girls that I often compared myself to them, and insecurity preyed on my self-esteem—especially being told that at 125 pounds, I had to lose more weight. My mother agreed. By fourteen, I was already an honorary member of Weight Watchers.

Anat and I continued to hang around quite a bit. She adored Ivan, and the three of us became inseparable. Ivan was kind to Anat. He included her in everything we did. He even tried to fix her up with one of his friends, but she wanted nothing to do with boys. Ivan would tease her, and their conversation would go like this:

"Anat, I think you and Chris would make a cute couple."

"I'm not interested in boys. How many times do I have to tell you, Ivan?"

"Do you think he's cute? He told me he thinks you're pretty."

"Stop! I don't care if he is cute or whether he thinks I'm pretty. I'm not interested in him or any other boy, for that matter."

And then the next time the three of us got together, the conversation almost verbatim would repeat.

The hurt I had experienced with losing Donna had finally waned with my growing friendship with Anat. I didn't think of Donna during the day as much as when she'd appear in a dream, leaving me with an empty feeling when I awoke. I had wanted to teach Donna how to knit, but our friendship ended before I had the chance. So, I decided to teach Anat, one of the greatest skills, if not the only one, my mother taught me.

As a young child, I watched the yarn dance gracefully around, between, under, and over my mother's needles until the first glimpse of an afghan, scarf, or sweater would emerge. There were times when she would have rows and rows completed, stop what she was doing, and with a perplexed look on her face, scan the *Good Housekeeping* pattern and her project. Letting out a sigh, she'd rip it all out and begin again. I remember asking her one day, "Why can't you leave that tiny mistake? No one will notice it."

"Because knitting is one of the few things in life you get to do over and over again. And even if no one else notices the mistake, you'll know it's there. The nagging feeling that someday someone will notice will haunt you like a bad dream. Besides, if you want to be a good knitter, you cannot get upset about a redo."

I knew I didn't want any bad dreams sticking around in my head, especially like the ones I'd had of King Kong when I was younger. It took only one time watching *King Kong* for that huge ape to pay regular visits to me in my dreams. The dreams, or more appropriately named night terrors, repeated in the same manner when they occurred. A loud alarm sounds. A sound loud enough to wake up the dead. I panic. A voice comes over a megaphone: "Citizens of New Haven, heed the warning: King Kong is coming to our city. Everyone is cautioned to take cover, hide wherever you can, because he will destroy everything in his path!"

As the nightmare unfolds, it squeezes the life out of me, and I can hardly breathe. My mother is not around—as usual. I must do this alone. Plan my escape on my own. I feel insignificant in the grandness of what is unfolding. I run as fast as I can through the streets of New Haven, looking for the perfect hiding place. The cacophony of screams from the herds of people was almost too much to bear. I run in and out of narrow spaces. I perspire furiously under the heat of the day, my breath dry, choking me as I desperately try to find cover. *Why is no one helping me?* I was invisible and alone.

"Run, run, Debbie, as fast as you can!" I hear what sounds like my mother and I am relieved that she was there to protect me . . . but, in all the confusion, it is *not* my mother—it is Azzie, my only protector. I can hear her, but I can't see her. Then . . . I see him, King Kong, larger than life, towering over all the buildings. *Has he spotted me yet? Is he coming for me? Yes, he's after me.* I run for what seems like forever, ready to collapse from utter exhaustion. I slip into the tiniest of spaces where I pray for safety. I take a deep breath, come into a state of wakefulness, relieved and exhausted. I realize it was all just a bad dream.

As much as there is no correlation between King Kong and knitting, the repetition of night terrors reminded me of a knitting pattern with its sequence of rows that would repeat again and again. And now that my mother convinced me that if I leave an error in one of my projects, I will have nightmares, I envision a giant ball of yarn following me around New Haven until it winds tightly around me and swallows me up—no do-over this time. Let me just make one thing very clear: From that day forward, I have never knowingly left a mistake in one of my patterns, even if it meant unraveling a few feet of an afghan that was just about completed.

Anat caught on to knitting at rapid speed, even when it came to winding the yarn into a ball. We took turns holding the yarn taut between our two wrists while the other rolled it up into a ball. We laughed so loud when one of us would drop the ball and it would spin out of control, leaving behind a knotted mess. The two of us got quite good at making scarves, so we decided to sell them. After deducting the cost of yarn, we made a whopping fifty cents apiece in profit, enough to buy a movie ticket, or a visit to Mr. Mooney's candy shop, where we could buy candy cigarettes, candy necklaces, or atomic fireballs, and still have plenty of change. Between the local candy shops and the candy in our house, I was sure to visit my dad's office regularly. Not exactly the kind of visit I welcomed.

I made sure I taught Anat the same lesson my mother had passed on to me. I carefully weaved the same story my mother told me about leaving in mistakes. I surely didn't want Anat to have night terrors. I remember the first time she found a mistake around eight inches back in a scarf she was making. "Oh my! What is this way back here?" she wailed.

"It's a mistake," I said matter-of-factly, as if it was something to be expected.

"And what am I supposed to do about it?" she asked.

"You have to unravel the pattern back to the point of the mistake and redo it."

"What!" Now she was visibly upset. Her eyes widened, and she abruptly threw down the scarf.

"Anat, listen to me," I said while laughing at how loud she screamed. Remembering my mother's words, I elaborated even more on what she'd said. "Knitting is one of the only things in life that you can do over and over again. Most mistakes cannot be undone. You get to make this right. And besides, if you leave that mistake in, even if no one else notices, you will always, always know it's there. It will haunt you in your dreams. Is that what you want?"

"Oh, okay," she said, succumbing to my wishes. "I'll rip the whole damn thing out."

In the same vein as a night terror was a visit to my father's dental office. One would think that having a father as a dentist would hold some benefits, such as free dental work or priority treatment. Free dental did come with the territory, but priority treatment fell short on many levels. To put it mildly, I was petrified to have to morph from a daughter to a patient. Although I loved helping in his office, which I did many summers, the dental chair was the last place I wanted to plant my behind.

Nothing was redeeming about a visit to Daddy's office. The glaring light he used to navigate my mouth caused halos of large white circles to project from my eyes. The drill played the drums on my heart every time it sped up as he depressed the pedal on the floor. And the worst part of all was the damn Novocain needle. I'd watch the intention on his face as he flicked the needle once, then twice, until a few drops of the fluid spurted out. My eyes widened and my mouth clamped down as the drill entered my mouth, making my father's job a lot harder.

Every time I'd resist his moves, he'd curtly demand, "Hold still." Then, he'd let out a loud puff of air that left his cheeks inflated like two balloons and continue with, "Now open as wide as you can. You'll feel a little prick." There was nothing "little" that went with a prick from a Novocain needle, especially when after the first one another one came and another one and another one. The only positive thing about being pricked six to eight times with a needle was that after two to three pricks, you were starting to get numb.

The worst day of my life in his dental chair was the time the Novocain did not take effect, and as he was drilling, a lightning bolt struck my mouth. He had hit a nerve. I grabbed the arms of the chair, jerked backward as my chest puffed out, and then my right leg flung forward without any warning, like an uncontrollable reflex, and hit him right in the balls. The last thing I remember my father saying as he abruptly moved about to prepare another Novocain needle was, "God damn it!"

That was the last day I went to my father's office, and by the time I was eighteen years old, I had lost two molars. I would mask my toothache pain by loading up with aspirin until the infection became so severe that I had to see an oral surgeon for extraction, who just so happened to be my mother's youngest brother. Thankfully, I matured enough to realize I needed to take care of my teeth.

~ ~ ~

When I wasn't spending time with Ivan or Anat or knitting, I was either babysitting for Laurie and her husband, Harvey, or the Rothbergs. The Rothbergs, really cool, with-it people, lived next door. I adored their baby boy, and any baby I laid eyes on I loved. From the time I was a young girl, I dreamed of having babies of my own, and some of those dreams came in bizarre ways. I can still remember the one when I was nine years old. Someone had left a basket on my doorstep, and in it was the most adorable baby. Excitedly, I swooped up the basket, ran to my mother, and shrieked, "Look what I found! Can I keep it? Please, pretty please? I'll take care of it all by myself." Shortly after my mother declared yes, I woke up realizing it was only a dream. I had many dreams like this over the years, and I still remember the disappointment that lingered after they ended.

Saturday night was approaching, and I had a date to babysit for the Rothbergs and have Ivan over again, with their permission. By now, I had proven to them I was trustworthy. I showed up on time, and they loved the way I cared for their son, so they agreed Ivan could come over after the baby was asleep. The plan was for Ivan to come at 9:00 P.M. I had bathed the baby at eight, read him a story, gave him a bottle, and put him down to sleep by 8:30. I waited with bated breath, pacing the floor several times and looking at the clock to will its hands to move faster. I peed several times and checked myself out in the mirror. I peeked out the back door where Ivan always entered to avoid any neighbors seeing him. My heart raced with the mounting anticipation until he finally arrived.

We settled into our favorite spot on the living room floor cushioned with a throw blanket. It was a warm night in early May, and I could still feel the dampness and sweat on Ivan's skin from his two-mile walk, which usually took forty-five minutes to an hour. I loved being in his arms. We talked about so much that night, especially about our dreams of getting married and having children. We talked about baby names, both boy and girl. There was nothing else that mattered in the world. It was Ivan and me, and we could conquer the world together. When we exhausted our words, we began to kiss. He was such a good kisser, his full lips so soft and sensual against mine, his manly cologne intoxicating.

"I love you so much, Rabbit," he said, groaning.

I loved the nickname Rabbit. He'd given it to me because he thought I had a cute nose. Can't blame him.

"I know you do, and I love you more," I replied.

His kisses continued along my neck until he found my nipples, playfully sucking and licking, moving back and forth between the two. As he made his way down toward my stomach, gently kissing along the way, my back arched and I groaned. Then finally, parting my hairs with his mouth, he found the softness of my swollen flesh. The pleasure escalated with the rise and fall of my pelvis until I finally exploded. Then, Ivan slid his body up until I felt his hardness gently slip inside me.

"Don't forget to pull out before you cum," I whispered.

Our bodies danced to the rhythm as we melted into each other until I heard his intense groan of pleasure. As he pulled out of me, he said, "Oh, shit! I don't think I pulled out completely before I came."

We lay next to each other, our unspoken words powerful in their silence. Worry consumed me. The tightness in my chest was almost unbearable. Thoughts of pregnancy, babies—the ones I adored so much—and abortion flooded my mind. Who would I tell? Who *could* I tell?

From that day on, the thought of getting my period consumed me. It was due a little over two weeks from the night we were together, smack dab in the middle of my cycle—not a good thing. I went about my days with the end of the school year a month away. The calendar on my desk marked "period" on May 26 spoke volumes as it peered back at me. With each "X" I marked in the box preceding the twenty-sixth, my heart skipped a few beats. I was either a day early or on time each month, and when the tender breasts I usually got a few days before my period seemed to have escaped me, thoughts of the inevitable overwhelmed me. And then May 26 arrived and left with no signs of my period. All other months, I would think to myself, *Oh, crap, it's that time of the month again.* This month, I prayed for blood to be bestowed upon me. I rang Ivan that night.

"I'm afraid I have some bad news," I said, the tears breaking through my words. "I'm usually not late and now I'm officially a day late. There's nothing we can do now. It's way too early for a pregnancy test and after calling Planned Parenthood, they said there's a minimum two-week waiting period."

"Okay," he said. "Make the appointment, and I'll pay for it and go with you."

His tone was steady and even, so nonchalant, so cool. Was he in complete denial, or was he just accepting the inevitable?

While nearly choking on my saliva, I agreed halfheartedly. "Yeah, sure, Ivan."

"We'll get through this together. Don't worry," he said.

We said our goodbyes and hung up. I sat in my room, alone in my thoughts. Ivan's words—We'll get through this together. Don't worry—repeated like a broken record. My imagination swirled with all kinds of thoughts. I lay in my bed and stared aimlessly at the ceiling, wishing the answers would suddenly appear before me. Most of all, I wondered what "we'll get through this together" meant.

Chapter 7

A woman called my name. She handed me a new patient form to complete, and I sat back down next to Ivan. I filled out the form and checked out the room as if looking for a sign to indicate I was in the right place. The waiting room was stark-white with nothing on the walls except a huge sign above the reception window that said Planned Parenthood League of Connecticut, I assumed just in case we forgot where we were. I wondered why a place that provided such bad news to kids like me didn't have cheerier decor on their walls, or maybe some signs such as We Are Here to Help, or The Choice Is Yours, or better yet, You Fucked Up, Dumbass Kid.

I returned the completed form and waited nervously for my name to be called again, my right leg bouncing in an uncontrollable up-and-down motion. Even though Ivan and I were together in that room, I was alone, and a part of me was royally pissed off at him for not being more careful that evening. *Damn you, Ivan. I'm the one who has to go through all this. Fuck you, fuck you, fuck you.* The piped-in classical music was an annoying and lousy choice for most teenagers, although playing songs such as Tim Hardin's "How Can We Hang On to a Dream?" might not work, either.

I grabbed a brochure titled "History of Birth Control" from a table, thinking I could lessen my nerves if I read. I opened it up, and my eyes went to a paragraph that read: "According to ancient Greek mythology, the goddess of spring, Persephone, refused to eat anything but pomegranate seeds after she was stolen from her mother, raped by the god of death, and kidnapped to the underworld. Medical historians now know why she only ate pomegranate seeds, which became one of the first oral contraceptives." For a moment, I laughed to myself as I remembered all those pomegranates I ate with my daddy. He had loved them and taught me how to eat those messy fruits with their blood-colored juices. *Hmmm, I guess instead of eating the fruit, I should have swallowed a whole bunch of seeds!* I thought.

Snapping me out of messy pomegranate thoughts, I overheard a conversation between a mother and her daughter sitting a few seats down from us. The mother was consoling her daughter while she held her hand. "Sweetie, everything is going to be fine. As long as you stay strong, we can get through this. Remember, I am here for you and will help you through this every step of the way."

A deep sense of sadness overwhelmed me as I watched that girl who appeared to be a few years younger than me. I knew, though, she was in good hands, but an intense longing pierced through my heart when I realized I would never have that kind of relationship with my mother. I wanted to magically change what I had with my mother into that same beautiful, caring one I witnessed. After all, if that happened, everything could be better—*would* be better—with her by my side . . . or, at least, I imagined it might be.

A ding-dong chime sounded, and a couple walked in. The girl, who appeared to be close to my age or a bit older, signed in. She was handed the new patient form to complete. When they sat down, her boyfriend put his arm around her shoulders and kissed her on her temple. I peered over at Ivan, who was engrossed in a lame gun magazine obviously placed in the waiting room for all the sperm shooters. Then I thought back to that first night Ivan and I were together at the Rothbergs' house before the night my life had changed in what felt like forever.

~ ~ ~

We faced each other on the floor, legs braided together like a pretzel. It was hard to tell where his limbs began and mine ended. Our arms cradled one another, and his warmth melted me like I was butter on a hot stove. Nothing else in the world mattered.

"I love you," Ivan whispered.

"Me too," I replied, hugging him tighter until I lost my breath and let it out like a burst balloon.

It was the first time we had ever uttered those three magical words.

"Can you imagine what beautiful kids we'll have one day? Ivan Junior!" he shouted, laughing.

I giggled too and nodded in agreement. I wanted to say so much more, but my gut told me not to. The excitement kept me trapped in silence. I could hear the beating of his heart with the rise and fall of his chest. A tear trickled out of the side of my eye and down the left side of my face. My emotions danced around in my head like some crazy version of *The Nutcracker*. We had just finished making love. Ivan felt the wetness on my cheek and immediately looked concerned.

"Rabbit, are you crying? What's wrong? Aren't you happy?"

"I'm so happy, Ivan," I blurted. "I've never felt happier. You are so perfect. We're so perfect. I don't want anything to mess this up. I love you so much!" I may have sounded overly emotional, maybe even hysterical at that point, but his calm demeanor and kind tone soothed me.

"What could mess this—or us—up?" His words were as comforting as a warm, cozy blanket by a fireplace on a cold night. "Don't worry that pretty head of yours. I'll protect you. You have my word. And . . . here. I've got something for you that'll make you feel better."

He took off the ring on his finger and handed it to me, explaining, "This was my father's class ring. I want you to wear it."

I carefully removed the gold chain from around my neck. My hands trembled with excitement as I opened the clasp and added his ring to the tiny Italian horn and Jewish star charms. I suddenly morphed into a ridiculously shy and childlike girl. However, I decided to be brave and ask him that huge, difficult teenage question. "Does this mean we're going steady?"

"Yes, Rabbit. Of course. We're a couple," he confirmed, smiling broadly. He kissed me gently on my nose and then kissed each cheek, lingering on the space where the wetness of my tears of joy remained.

~ ~ ~

I heard a loud call of my name, usurping any and all sweet thoughts of that night with Ivan. "Deborah Barnett," the nurse practitioner announced. *God,* I thought, *how embarrassing. She couldn't have spoken louder if she had a megaphone at her mouth.* I got up, and Ivan barely took his eyes off the magazine.

"I'll be waiting right here for you."

Yeah, shithead, you'd better be. After all, this is your fuckin' fault!

I followed the nurse practitioner into a room. I noticed how well her stark-white, freshly pressed uniform matched the stark-white walls of the waiting room. Were they trying to tell us something? Give us some not-so-subtle reminder of how we fucked up, or a hint of the purity we'd left behind? The nurse practitioner handed me a small cup with a lid and a large, wrapped disinfectant wipe. In a warm, soft voice, she said, "If this is your first time, be sure to wipe from front to back before you pee into the cup."

My mouth and eyes opened wide. I wanted to make some wisecrack remark, but I kept my thoughts to myself. *Is she crazy? First time . . . you mean girls go through this more than once?* As she directed me to the bathroom, my hands held onto the small plastic cup as if it were a fragile glass ornament. Sitting on the toilet that was cold enough to give me freezer burn, I peed into the container. I sat there with my mouth agape while staring at the yellow liquid that would ultimately seal my fate. I placed the lid back on the cup and watched the liquid as it moved to the rhythm of my trembling hand. This was undoubtedly one trip to the bathroom I would never forget.

When I left the bathroom, she greeted me like a drill sergeant, eyeing the cup to make sure I performed my task. "You're all set for now, Debbie. We'll call you in a few days with the results."

"Okay," I said, my palms sweaty. "But please don't say where you are calling from if someone else answers the phone."

"We are always discreet," she said.

Wow, you guys have this all figured out, don't you? I thought.

Ivan met me at the checkout counter and pulled out cash to pay. I thanked him, and we left the building. He walked me back to the bus stop where we were both to take different buses home. "I'm going to walk home," he said uncharacteristically. "I need to clear my head." He gave me what I was sure was an obligatory kiss on the cheek.

Hmmm, that was as cold as ice, or maybe I'm just paranoid. Fuck you, I thought one last time before my thoughts of "what if?" swallowed me up in one big fucking piece.

Chapter 8

Two days later at 4:30, the telephone rang. The call came just in the nick of time. With my mother being out of the house, the phone call was impeccable.

"Is this Debbie?" I told her it was. "This is Planned Parenthood calling. We have your results back, and you are pregnant. Approximately four to five weeks along."

I couldn't decide if she thought she was delivering good news or bad news. The tone in her voice was somewhere between excitement and dread.

My throat tightened, and I could barely speak but managed to say thank you. Then I heard her say the unthinkable.

"If you need any help with what to do next . . . I mean, whether you want to keep the baby or give the child up for adoption . . . well, I can set up the appointment for you right now if you'd like."

If I'd like . . . Is she crazy? There is absolutely nothing to like about any of this. Thinking quickly, I blurted out, "No, I'll call back when I'm ready."

I hung up, and tears rushed down my cheeks. I screamed, "Oh, fuck!" I was sick to my stomach. The fear gripped me like a noose tightening around my neck. The thought of what my mother would do if she found out had my head spinning. If the beating a year ago was any indication, then my life was over. *Damn, you messed up this time!*

I paced in my room for what seemed like hours until the room was moving with me. And then I heard the signature horn from my mother's car, letting us know she needed help taking the groceries into the house. I took a deep breath, hoping to ease the pounding of my heart. I looked in the bathroom mirror to see if there were signs that I had been crying. There were. My eyes reminded me of a red fireball that let you see the white part only after your tongue endured the pain long enough to do so. Oh, yes, I was a dead giveaway with my eyes ablaze and blotches that made a not-so-pretty pattern from my cheeks to my chest.

Kenny and I helped take in the groceries. I kept my head down and away from my mother's gaze the entire time. When dinner was ready, most of the redness had subsided. I could barely get a mouthful of food down my throat and spit some food into my napkin while my mother and father weren't looking. Kenny's smirk and questioning nod indicated he saw me and was wondering what was going on. When I had most of my plate cleaned, I got up, excused myself, and disposed of the napkin, shoving it down into the bottom of the basket.

Once in my room, I lay in silence. I thought of putting on music to soothe my distress but couldn't get myself to reach for the knob on the transistor which now seemed far out of reach. I tossed and turned from left to right and placed my self-pitying face down on the pillow. For a moment, the thought of suffocating myself seemed like a better alternative. As I eyed the phone, I dreaded breaking the news to Ivan. Finally, I got up the nerve.

He answered, and I blurted out the news. There was dead silence for what seemed like hours. I finally spoke, my words flowing out as quickly as the tears that streamed down my cheeks and onto the receiver.

"What are we going to do now, Ivan? I can't get an abortion unless we get an illegal one. I overheard once that there are doctors who perform them illegally. It's expensive, but what other choice do we have?"

Roe vs. Wade, the 1973 Supreme Court decision that established a woman's right to legal abortion, was years from being enacted. I faced a remedy that was not only illegal, but it was hazardous—a pretty frightening decision for any young girl to meet. Unless, the only other options—like the Planned Parenthood nurse I knew was suggesting—I keep the baby or give it up for adoption. As much as I loved babies, I knew that keeping the baby wasn't possible, and besides, even if it were, neither of those options would ever get the *pass-go* approval from my mother.

After some more silence on his end, Ivan responded in a low, sullen tone, "Let me figure this out. I'm close to my dad. I can talk to him, and maybe he'll have an answer."

I hung up the phone, feeling as if I'd just lost something—not sure what, but I realized this was one of the first times our conversation did not end with "I love you."

On that following Saturday morning, Ivan called. I had been up since nine hoping to hear from him. Friday was the first time we did not speak on the phone, although we did see each other in school.

"Debbie, I have great news. When my father was in the army, he used to perform abortions. He said he could do this in our house."

His words bounced out of his mouth as if they were doing jumping jacks, and as bizarre and unfamiliar as the idea seemed, his words *father* and *army* were safe and comforting. I thought of my dad, who had also been in the army. He was drafted into the Dental Corps Medical Group of the 33rd Division after he graduated from Tuffs School of Dental Medicine. There, he practiced dentistry. And while the two professions were nothing alike, if performing abortions was even considered a business, there was one distinct similarity between them. While Ivan's dad was extracting unborn fetuses from women and girls, my dad was extracting teeth.

I winced at the thought, and my body tightened as I placed one hand on my cheek and the other on my abdomen. I reluctantly uttered, "Oh, God. Okay. Set it up as soon as possible."

We hung up, but those three precious words were still missing. Despite everything, my focus was ridding my body of the stain that would bring me shame. Nothing else mattered—*this* was my focus.

Later that day, Ivan called to confirm that June 26 at 9:00 A.M. would be the date and time. Although I had no idea what was in store for me, an enormous sense of relief streamed over me. Ivan had thought it'd be better if we did this after school ended on June 25, so the day after seemed to be the best.

The end of the school year approached with finals underway and summer fever in bloom. There was nothing like the feeling that went along with the anticipation of the last day of school. While others prepared for summer camp, my weekend seemed endless as I muddled through, keeping myself busy, trying desperately not to focus on the appointed day. When it arrived, I woke up at 6:00 a.m., showered, and cussed to myself. I nibbled at a perfunctory breakfast as I waited for my mother and father to leave. Then I successfully slipped out the front door.

As I walked to the Whalley Avenue bus line, I looked up to revere the pillow-like clouds in the sky. They were seemingly floating, creating interesting shapes. I thought I saw one that looked a lot like a mushroom, except that the top had eyes and what seemed to me like a smiling mouth. No nose. *I wished I could feel that free right now. How cool would that be? I'd be billowy, light, airy, and with a front-row seat to a gorgeous double rainbow after light showers had passed. And I'd be above the lightning, the storms, the scary stuff.*

I faintly heard a whoosh of doors closing. Jolted back to reality, the bus I'd boarded suddenly jerked, moving again. I was nauseated. Any more jerking, and I would barf all over that damn bus. One more stop. I was almost there.

But eff me. Freedom? Pfft. Rainbows, dreams, and drifting clouds? C'mon. I was fifteen. Knocked up. Bunny croaked. And how appropriate, after all, my nickname was Rabbit. But wait . . . Br'er Rabbit was a force to be reckoned with, and he was a whole lot smaller than me. Maybe I could come up with some ingenious ways to outsmart my state of affairs. Or perhaps I could transform myself into Peter Cottontail and go hopping down the croaked-up bunny trail. Neither Br'er Rabbit nor Peter Cottontail could help me now. I was pregnant and about to enter Ivan's house, where his army dad was going to help rid me of this "problem potentially." It was kind of nuts. But what other choice did I have since abortion was illegal?

I was screwed.

Onward. I rang the doorbell of Ivan's house. Even at this hour, the *diiing-dooong* seemed to reverberate through the desolate streets like a warning bell.

Within a skipped heartbeat, I watched the heavy door swing open. Before me stood a very tall, burly, middle-aged man, disheveled, and unshaven. I couldn't help but notice the distinct mismatched striped shirt and plaid pants. Was that a stain on his collar? A beer-belly gut? Great. Ivan had told me that I could trust his father to do this abortion and that he had done them when he was in the army. Honestly, though? Forgive me. His dad looked more like he had just gone dumpster-diving for food than any kind of doctor I had ever seen.

"Hi, Debbie. I'm Ivan's dad, Mr. Chovnik," he chimed brightly. "But you can call me Bogdan. Come on in."

Weird, I thought. We're not having tea.

Hesitantly, I stepped in, keeping my arms folded. I surveyed the room. Ivan, the supposed love of my life, was standing in the living room just to the right of the entryway.

"Uhhh . . . hey," he mumbled, oddly on edge. He appeared frozen in place as if he were the one getting ready to do this crazy-ass thing.

So much for my boyfriend calming me down. Jeez. What am I doing here? I passed by Ivan, unable to make eye contact, so I turned my head away. The disappointment festered in me like venom slowly eating away at me.

"Follow me," his dad said. "I've got everything set up in my bedroom."

Do you? The bedroom? Ugh. I forced a smile on my face without looking at him, hoping to hasten the throbbing in my chest. My mind wandered into a frightening, alternate universe, time-space chasm yawning and opening wide behind some trap door. If I hadn't known better, I would've thought I was starring in one of those *Twilight Zone* episodes. And I'd know. I'd seen enough episodes by now to be considered an expert. Now all I had to do was jump in and leave this world behind.

I dragged my feet in an uneven stride, following Ivan's dad, Bogdan, to the bedroom. For some reason, the flowery window curtains and matching bedspread seemed like a promising beacon of decent taste and a good sign. Maybe this would be okay. I immediately noticed a large white towel on the bed and a white sheet on top of it.

I scoffed. White. All white, waiting on the bed there for me. I was still innocent and naive yet pregnant. And something big was about to go down. There had to be some irony there.

At the foot of the bed was a small table. On it, some medical instruments, a bowl of water, and hand towels. Bogdan told Ivan to close the door and wait outside. Appearing almost grateful, he scuttled out like a nervous mouse. I desperately wanted to follow him.

"Get undressed from the waist down," Bogdan commanded. "Then, get under the sheet. I'll turn around. Let me know when you're done."

His matter-of-fact, sergeant-like tone pierced my body as if I were being stung by a thousand bees. The room suddenly closed in on me, and all I could see were shiny silver instruments lying on that small table. Lots of them in different sizes. Were those things going inside me? I placed my right hand over my crotch as if to protect it. If I had any idea that I would be in this predicament, I would have gladly worn a chastity belt! The thought of that made me snicker, and for a brief moment, I forgot what was ahead of me.

I did as I was told, lying half naked and staring up at the tray ceiling. In the middle was a gilded gold medallion with an intricate lace design surrounding the hanging light fixture. I was upon a strange bed, in a strange house, alone with Ivan's father. His company had not yet been comforting. My mind traced the details of the medallion as if looking for clues to escape the nightmare. I had no choice, right? This or nothing. Yet, the whole thing was freaking me out. Maybe I could click my ruby-red heels three times, be safe, and go home?

"I'm ready." My voice cracked barely above a whisper.

He arrived quickly to the foot of the bed, put his hands under the sheet, and spread my legs wide, bending my knees upward. I recoiled and resisted. Despite being alive, I think rigor mortis had set in.

"Shh. Shh. Relax, Debbie. I need to examine you before we begin. Hold still, please."

Hold still, please? Didn't Kaa, the python, tell Mowgli that as he was trying to strangle him?

My back jerked in an upward motion and then fell to the bed when I felt his finger go inside me. I had never thought of all the details. *Does Ivan have any idea what's going on here?*

"Listen," he told me sternly. "For me to do this properly, you need to lie still. You also need to be moist, and you aren't. If I penetrate you, it will help make you wet."

Wait! What? He was *Kaa! I knew it! Slimy, slithering snake! Demon! Benedict Arnold!* My mind yelled angrily, *Nooo!* But my mouth was paralyzed, shut down in fear, desperation, and confusion. This man was going to rape me. Rape me! And me? I was going to let him.

Make-believe you're somewhere else. You have no choice. Get this over with already.

He removed his pants, tossed away the sheet covering my body, and got on top of me. His large, protruding belly jiggled and swayed back and forth as he positioned himself. Now, his deeply creased jowls jutted out offensively in front of my face. I closed my eyes tightly—as I'd do during a horror film that frightened me—and then his penis plunged into me, once, twice, three, four, five times. His breathing was labored and heavy. Suddenly, I could feel his foul, sticky semen leak out of me as he collapsed and grunted.

Did that just happen?

Revolted and in shock, my flesh turned cold as I bristled beneath him. In despair, with my dignity shredded and torn, my entire body shivered in disgust. Then, as if he had just routinely brushed his teeth first thing in the morning, he got up matter-of-factly, put on his pants, and cheerily said, "Now, back to business." He had the nerve to smile.

Slimy bastard, I thought. *How dare you! Traitor! Rat! Odious, pathetic excuse for a human!* I yelled in my mind so loudly that my subconscious must have looked like a picture of *The Scream* by Edvard Munch.

I immediately grabbed the sheet to cover my naked, abused body. He brought over a small seat and sat at the end of the bed. Reaching under the sheet, he inserted one of those instruments into me that I had spied earlier.

"This is going to hurt, but there's nothing we can do about that," the snake told me. "I have to dilate your cervix to abort the fetus."

Just do it already.

I gripped the bedspread on both sides of me, clutching the only sign of real comfort. He started with the first instrument. Searing pain invaded my lower region. A second instrument went in as the first came out. He must have done this several times. I was in agony. I could hardly breathe, and I must have blacked out.

From far away, I heard the traitor say, "Oh, good." I was half-dazed, sweating, and barely conscious. "You're back with me, Debbie. You passed out for a short while. This cool cloth should help."

Kindness? Thanks, toad wart.

He placed a wet washcloth on my forehead and went back to the foot of the bed.

"We're just about done, Debbie. You're doing very well. Your cervix is fully dilated. When I insert this last instrument, it'll remove the fetus from you. You'll feel a pinching, but I promise to do this as quickly as possible."

Then, as if a knife were cutting away my insides, an unimaginable pain soared through me. It was excruciating. Torture. I let out a blood-curdling scream as an ocean of tears poured down my face.

"That's it, Debbie. All finished."

Good. Go away. Be gone before someone drops a house on you too. The pain lingered like a bad toothache, throbbing, and pulsating until any decency left was masked.

He handed me a package of Kotex overnight sanitary napkins as if he were giving me a congratulatory gift of sorts instead of standard feminine pads and instructed me to wear one before getting dressed. Still covered with the sheet, I stood up awkwardly, feeling weak and more nauseated than ever before. My gait was as unsteady as a newborn giraffe trying to walk for the first time. Wiping the tears from my eyes, I got dressed without exposing myself, using the sheet as a useless hideout fort.

"You might feel some cramping later and have some bleeding, but by tomorrow, you should be just fine," the snake said.

I left the bedroom, noting the clock next to the credenza on the way out. It was noon. I walked past Ivan, sitting on the sofa in the living room. He looked a little shaken up and possibly weirded out. Maybe he was sad. I couldn't even look him in the eye, especially after what had just happened. I only wanted to escape. Flee. How could I ever tell him the truth? I would probably ruin his life, or his father's marriage, I guess. There were no thoughts of me or my life being ruined because I deserved this. I had gotten myself into this. I was damaged now. Broken. And I was done. We were done. Everything was done. I mumbled a goodbye, turned on my heel, and left.

The walk to the bus stop, the bus ride home, and the walk home were grueling. I was weak, both emotionally and physically. I was defeated. I thought Ivan's father was helping me—helping us—but how could that be after what he had done? I wanted to crawl into a ball and pretend this was all a bad dream. I arrived at home a little after 1:00 P.M. I grabbed a Tab from the refrigerator and headed up to my bedroom. I showered and scrubbed my body hard, wishing for the pain of the day to swirl down the drain. Feeling a bit better after the shower, I put on one of those overnight pads, a freebie from Mr. Chovnik for my good deeds, and some fresh clothes. Then I stretched out on top of my bed. My mother was playing mah jongg that afternoon. After what I had been though, I didn't want to see her. I started feeling some cramping, so I got up, took a few aspirin, and lay back down. I must have dozed off for hours. I remembered waking up to my mother, calling us down for dinner.

"Kenny, can you tell Mommy I'm not feeling well? Tell her I'll get something to eat later." Barely able to keep my head off the pillow, I fell right back to sleep.

I think it was around 9:00 p.m. when I woke up shivering and in a pool of blood. The blood had poured through the Kotex like a failed dam, spewing down my legs and onto my sheets. I was in agony! I yelled for Kenny, who was just a room away.

"What's the matter?" I could hear the concern in his voice as he bolted into my room.

"Quick, go tell Mommy I'm bleeding badly and am in terrible pain. I think I need to go to the emergency room. Ask her to call Harvey. He'll explain everything." Harvey was my sister's husband, who had become a confidant. I had told him about the pregnancy. He was the only one besides Ivan who knew of the abortion. He promised not to mention it to a soul, but thinking back on it now, I would have been better off if he betrayed my confidence. He could have saved my dumb ass from the sign outside Mr. Chovnik's house that I missed, which read Free Abortions: Enter at your own risk.

Kenny flew out of my room and stampeded down the staircase. Minutes later, my mother was in my room.

"I spoke to Harvey; for God's sake," she said. "Why didn't you come to me?"

Really? Go to you? When would that ever happen?

"Do we have to discuss that now?" I was groaning. "Can you please just get me to the hospital?"

She yelled for Kenny to grab a large towel. She handed it to me and told me to put it between my legs.

My parents and Kenny led me out to our station wagon. I sprawled out in the back seat, my father driving, my mother in the passenger seat, and Kenny in the cargo area. I moaned and screamed the whole ride there.

"Hurry, please! It's bad—really bad!"

"Your father is driving as fast as he can. We don't want to get into an accident on our way," my mother shouted.

Twenty minutes later, we pulled up to the emergency room door at St. Raphael's Hospital. We hurried into the waiting room.

"Hurry!" she shrilled, slamming her fists down even harder. "Do you hear me? My daughter is bleeding badly, and she needs help right now." By this point, her eyes bulged out, and her face was void of color as if she had just received a visit from a vampire.

Before I knew it, the candy striper, a young girl in her teens, assisted me into a wheelchair and whisked me away. The pain jolted through me as she sped down the hallway. Once in the emergency room, the nurses appeared and were moving quickly around me.

"Can I get something for the pain, please?" I asked through my tears. My hands clenched my abdomen, and my face contorted into a grimace with each deep breath I inhaled.

"We are going to give you something through the IV to relax you, but we cannot give you anything too strong," one of the nurses replied. "The doctors need you to be awake through everything. They want to be sure you don't go into septic shock."

"Please," I said, "can you call my sister Laurie? I need her. Please."

"Sure, honey," she said. "I'll go talk to your mother in a minute as soon as we get you ready for the doctor."

Then I heard the nurse say to another nurse, "That poor, poor child. This is a botched abortion if I ever saw one."

What did I do to myself? Are they pitying me, or is it because I'm in danger of something worse? Please, God, help me—I promise I will do better from now on if you just help me.

Tubes were now dangling from my arm, machines beeping to the rhythm of my heart. I was groggy, and the piercing discomfort had subsided just enough for me to handle the pain. A familiar touch sent a warm, comforting feeling up my arm. I turned and saw Laurie by my side.

"Oh, Debbie, what have you done? You could have called me," she said softly.

One of the nurses moved to the back of my bed and said to Laurie, "We've got to get her to the operating room now. We have no time to waste."

Laurie kissed me on the forehead.

"I'll be waiting for you when you get into recovery." They wheeled me into the operating room in a speedy but careful fashion. The last thing I remembered before slipping into unconsciousness was a nurse by my side saying, "Count backward from ten."

So, I did.

Later, I regained consciousness. I was in the recovery room. The first person I saw was Laurie standing by my side.

"Hey, how are you feeling?" She rubbed my arm to comfort me.

"I'm okay," I said, hardly able to get my voice out, jittering from the anesthesia.

"You know, the doctor said you are one lucky girl. You were closer to death than any of us imagined. That man your mother told us about, who I'd like to kill myself, left a piece of the placenta in you along with using possible unsterilized instruments, and you became septic. The doctor said that by the time you came in, the infection was so bad that the next thing would have been organ failure—and possible death."

As quickly as we fell in love, as beautiful as our days together, it was over between Ivan and me. A whirlwind romance that, as many young breakups do, ended in hurt. I never forgot my conversation with Ivan the first night we made love and the excitement of going steady for the first time—and the nickname, Rabbit, he'd given me would remain an indelible piece of my existence.

The tears of joy that ran down my cheeks that day left an indelible mark on my being and one that would remind me of that fateful day and how it became a part of who I am for years to come. My mother made it clear that what happened that day or what led up to that day would never be mentioned again. So, I buried its poison deep inside where reason met absurdity. Those wounds and shame would follow me around, leaving the door open for others to slip in.

Chapter 9

I rarely spent quality time with my mom, except for our trips to the weekly Weight Watchers meetings—if one would consider this quality time. My mother was already a lifetime member, the term given to those who reached their goal weight and stayed within a few pounds of that weight. By the time I was nearing fifteen, I had joined and rejoined the Weight Watchers colony many times. Whenever ten pounds latched its way onto my young frame, my mom was eager to sign me up again.

I was twelve when she first convinced me to join. She was mortified by my excess pounds, as if I were teetering on blubber whale status. Our appearance and what others thought were a high priority for my mom. My first trip was mortifying.

~ ~ ~

"Maaaahhhm . . ." The word stretched out of my mouth like a rubber band about to burst at any moment. "Why do I have to go?"

"Because I said so," she nodded in affirmation with those famous last words so often heard throughout my childhood. "And besides," she continued, "if we don't get that weight of yours under control, there will be no turning back."

"Gosh, Mom, you make it sound like I'm a blimp." I lowered my head, touched my stomach, and scanned my body, trying to convince myself I was wasn't a blimp.

Pointing and waving her index finger at me, she said with an annoying tone in her voice, "You're not a blimp, but if we don't get you on a diet soon, you will be."

Defeated, I mouthed, "Oh, all right." I stomped my foot on the ground and huffed my way to the car. I wasn't going to win this battle—not that I ever had with her.

As we drove to the meeting, I peered out the passenger window, trying to imagine the meeting. *Oh my goodness, what if they make me undress before they weigh me?* I cracked each knuckle one by one until my mother shouted,

"Stop that. You're going to cause your knuckles to grow. Do you want that, young lady?"

I didn't respond, but I did stop cracking them. I certainly didn't want my knuckles to have to lose weight too.

We pulled up to the Weight Watchers location, which was in a strip mall not far from our house. The front of the bay was all glass, and I could see a crowd of women standing around talking. We walked into one large room with a sign-in desk and a large doctor's scale behind a partition. I looked around and noticed there was not one man there. I had never really thought about it, but I was curious as to whether men didn't get fat or if they did, why was it okay for them? There was something to that, and my twelve-year-old mind wanted desperately to figure that one out.

We were next in line when I heard the lady behind the table call my mother's name. "Hi, Mollye, how did your week go?"

"Well, we will certainly find out as soon as I step on that scale. We attended a bar mitzvah this past weekend, so I'm hoping the numbers aren't too bad."

"Okay, hop on."

My mother slid off her Capezio shoes and stepped onto the scale. I exhaled, relieved to see I wasn't going to strip.

The check-in lady slid the bar to my mother's last recorded weight and then slowly moved it one way and then the other way. "Not too bad, Mollye. It looks like you've put on only two pounds this week. You'll take that off in no time. You're staying for the meeting, aren't you?"

"Yes, of course." My mother got off the scale and looked my way. She raised her eyebrows and widened her bottom lip, indicating disappointment and embarrassment. After all, she was supposed to be setting an example for me.

She turned back to the check-in lady and boasted, "By the way, I'd like you to meet my daughter Debbie. I want to sign her up today."

"Welcome. We are pleased to have you join us!" the lady said gleefully. "Please fill this out while I take payment from your mother." I was expecting her to say, "Wait! You can't join. You don't have enough weight to lose." But she didn't; instead, I placed one hand over my stomach to mask the bulge while the other hand took the form from her.

After I returned the completed form to the lady, she said, "Hop on the scale."

I followed suit and kicked off my white Dr. Scholl's sandals. "Okay, let's see what we have here."

Jeez . . . she isn't going to announce this to the whole world, is she? I wanted to flee the scene right then and there. Escape. Poof. Be gone. Then, I let out a huge breath as I watched her write down my weight on the form I had completed, and in a space marked Goal, she wrote "84 lbs." Based on the number I had seen on the scale, I had to lose a whopping fourteen pounds. Dang. I would never be able to lose that kind of weight. Nonetheless, I embarked on my journey to lose weight and stayed out of the famous Curtis Drive "candy cabinet" located in my very own house.

Holding a new-member welcome kit, I took a seat next to my mom with the rest of the women waiting to hear the lecture. I checked out every inch of the room. At the front was a large stand with one of the most enormous pads of paper I'd ever seen. On it were different foods and caloric values. At the top was a hand drawing of a piece of meat about the size of my palm, and next to it was an equal sign followed by "160 cal." There were several items on the list, and at the bottom was a horizontal line under the list of calories and then "1,200 cal. total" was written. I didn't know what calories were, but I guessed I would soon find out.

The room started filling up. Once all seats were occupied, women had to stand at the back of the room. The stares penetrated me like claws digging into my skin. I was the youngest person in the room and, by far, the smallest. *Nah, it's just my imagination. You aren't that important.* Then, I felt a tap at my shoulder and turned around.

"What in the world are you doing here?" a brutish woman said. "You don't have enough weight to lose."

"Uh . . . uh . . . I'm. . ." Struggling to find an answer, my mother quickly interjected.

"Leave her alone, why don't you! It's none of your business whether she has weight to lose or not."

The rude woman raised her nose in the air and turned back around. I lowered myself in my seat, slumped my shoulders, and sat motionless for the rest of the meeting. I listened to the leader motivate the audience and give out little badges to those who met specific goals. I didn't want to draw any attention to myself or be subject to any more embarrassment. And then the unthinkable happened. The leader announced, "All new members, please stand so we can welcome you." I flat out wanted to die—crumble to pieces, just like the topping from Drake's Cakes, which were partially to blame for my sitting in this room.

"Go on, Debbie, get up."

"Mom . . . no," I said, raising my brow and as wide-eyed as a deer.

"For God's sake, get up." She raised her voice as she pushed me up.

I stood like a soldier under command. I wanted to see how many other new members stood among the group, but my head was locked in a forward position.

"Everyone, give our new members a big round of applause," the leader announced.

A loud round of applause sounded in the room. I wanted to cover my ears and make it stop. I could hear the women laughing in silence through their stares. The smirk on their faces said it all. I was a mockery. My legs started to wobble under me, and my stomach rumbled. I knew if I didn't sit down soon, I'd either faint or… the unthinkable. I peered over at the bathroom with that thought in mind just in case I needed to make a beeline for it.

Where was Underdog when I needed him? He certainly wasn't off to save *my* day.

Just in the nick of time, I heard the greatest words ever spoken: "You can all sit down now."

Later that day, I was in and out of the kitchen, eyeing the candy cabinet. I was a one-person marching band with my hands on my hips. I'd march in, turn to the candy cabinet, stop and stare, and then reluctantly turn around, arms swinging at my sides as I marched out.

It wouldn't have been so tempting, the 83 Curtis Drive "candy cabinet," but this was not any ole candy cabinet. This was the best darn candy cabinet on the entire street or maybe in the whole neighborhood. It was Gary's, Kenny's, and my go-to place as soon as we got home from school or a place we frequented on the weekends. The cabinet was home to several things. At any given time, you might find nonpareils, M&M's (both regular and peanut), Hershey's chocolate candy bars, Twizzlers, Charleston Chews, Chips Ahoy! chocolate chip cookies, Oreos, and, one of my dad's favorites, Mallomars.

There it was in plain sight, staring at me and tempting me. I was torn between good and evil—just like Eve. Waiting for me inside the cabinet were lots and lots of forbidden fruit. *Hah . . . but only if they were some kind of fruit. According to Weight Watchers, I could partake at least once a day.*

My journey to lose weight was certainly not without challenge by any means, let alone with the candy my mother so diligently kept stocked in the cabinet. How did she think I was going to lose weight with that kind of junk in the house? I mean, really. It was a cruel form of punishment for any young girl. I might as well have been locked up somewhere safe away from the throes of the sugar monsters.

By the time I started high school at age fourteen, I had shed all my weight physically, but the young, overweight girl who sat in on many Weight Watchers meetings became a part of me. No matter how thin I was, I was never thin enough. Thin became my obsession, and it ate away at me like a cruel and unjust punishment. If ten pounds crept back on me after I allowed the temptation of the candy cabinet to demonize me, I'd be right back at the overweight club. Eventually, being "thin enough" became synonymous with my self-esteem; the self-esteem—or should I say, lack thereof—that stemmed from the little praise (if any) I heard from my mother. But I would work hard so that others would make me feel important.

Chapter 10

I was mesmerized by its beauty as it sat on the easel. The setting sun cast a shadow on the strong yet seraphic features of the face. The hair flowed loosely along the youthful breasts; the nipples peeked out from beneath. There was a strong, confident young girl staring back at me. In silence, she spoke to me through the depth of her eyes. Who was this girl looking back at me?

~ ~ ~

I was entering tenth grade and wanted to begin anew, start fresh, and feel like a typical teenager. I was mostly excited to have art class this year, especially since my dad loved art, and I seemed to have inherited some of his artistic genes. Family and close friends admired his art, and although he was not an acclaimed artist, he was very talented. The walls of our house were tastefully decorated with his works that included acrylics, oils, charcoals, and wood carvings.

When he was not at his dental office, and as far back as I can remember, he could be found working on a project in the basement. I was so proud of his art and eager to point it out to anyone who came into our house. Although many times he was approached to sell his works, that idea did not interest him. He preferred to keep his treasures and joy of painting within the family.

The details of some of his wood carvings were incredible. Today, when I pass "The Dentist" hanging on my wall, I imagine my dad chiseling away at the wood, millimeter by millimeter, with such precision. My father crafted this piece while practicing dentistry in the army. It depicts a patient leaning backward on a dentist, while one of the assistant's arms is securely hooked to the patient's right arm and her free hand offering additional support. His furrowed brow and tightly closed eyes show fear and angst, indicative of the times when anesthesia was not used. I was always amazed, knowing that with one wrong move, there was no going back. His artwork was dispersed among the six kids after he died.

I could hardly wait for art class, which was my last class of the day. From the moment I first laid my eyes on Mr. Kurk, he was as I imagined an art teacher would look. He had a head of dark, curly hair that hung scraggly around his neck. He had an undeniably pretentious way of strutting around the room. Cool and confident. The only thing missing from his artful appearance was a beret, which would have been a dead giveaway. He was not tall and carried a few extra pounds spread evenly over his body.

I excelled in Mr. Kurk's class, taking on any task or project he assigned with diligence and perseverance. The other students often admired my work and commented on my ability. I often helped others not as skilled in art. Before long, it was apparent I was the teacher's pet.

As the year went on, Mr. Kurk gave me extra credit assignments, and I gladly took them. Whenever I could, I offered to stay and wash the brushes and water cups and dispose of the brown paper covering the large wooden art desk that sat in the center of the room. Mr. Kurk was just the cure I needed for the lack of self-esteem that weighed heavily on mind since home life proved empty of praise and full of criticism.

My mother still reminded me regularly when I needed to take off a few pounds. I started feeling more and more self-conscious of my body image even when others saw me as the thinnest at Weight Watchers.

Helping Mr. Kurk was a no-brainer for me. Inside his classroom, I was impenetrable and free from criticism. I walked around with my head high and back erect. I had swag in my walk that exuded a strong, proud girl filled with confidence.

Audrey Korrick, a girl I had met in Hebrew Day, was also in my art class. We hung around a lot that year. Audrey was a thin, tiny-built girl who was not very pretty and a tad on the homely side. She had been diagnosed with regional ileitis, caused by Crohn's disease, which obstructed her small intestines. The illness, as I remember, was harrowing, and she had to succumb to many surgeries to resection or removal of the diseased areas. The pain she endured was, and still is, something I will never forget. I'm not sure if Audrey's illness kept her from having friends, but it didn't keep me away. Not being one of the popular girls or having been subject to false rumor, I continued to gain a sense of compassion and empathy for the underdog, and that underdog at this time was Audrey. Besides, I didn't have many friends, either, so the two of us became inseparable. I may not have been one of the popular girls, but in Audrey's eye, I was special—and that worked for me. Audrey often stayed to helped me cleanup for Mr. Kurk, but on this particular day, she had a doctor's appointment, so I stayed alone.

Busily, I cleared the brown paper covering from the table and took several trips to the sink, emptied the water cups, and placed the brushes in the sink to be washed. The room was eerily quiet when it was just Mr. Kurk and me. I stopped periodically to look at the students' paintings that hung around the room, and noticed mine. There was no doubt that I was my daddy's daughter. I glanced over at Mr. Kurk, who was busy at his desk, probably preparing for his next day's class. He spotted me looking at him and gave me a coy glance back.

I made my way over to the sink and started cleaning the brushes. When I was just about done with the last brush, I heard footsteps behind me, and then a warm poof of air made its way to my right cheek. Without notice, Mr. Kurk moved aside my full head of blonde hair and lightly kissed me on the neck. I jerked in surprise, yet there was something tingly and warm about his kiss. I turned, thinking I could slip to the side, but by the time I was face-to-face with him, he embraced me.

"Oh, Debbie," he whispered. "You are incredibly beautiful. You take my breath away." I fell silent under his trance. I did not feel the abuse of power that overcame me. I was, at that moment, a special girl, a delicate, handpicked flower. There was something I trusted in Mr. Kurk. He was my tenth-grade art teacher, well-liked from all appearances. Before I knew it, we were on the floor, and he was rubbing himself up and down the length of my body. His penis felt hard, and the pressure of his movements on my pubic bone hurt. Then, he moved my panties to one side and slid in. He continued his movements, faster in pace with his breathing until he fell on top of me. *What just happened? I guess he came. Boy, that was quick.* I turned my head to one side, catching a glimpse of one of my paintings, a reminder that I was still in art class.

    We both got up. I straightened out my slacks and gulped loud enough for him to hear. My index finger awkwardly tapped at my lips while my eyes looked anywhere but at his. I wondered what had just happened and whether it was right or wrong. I walked quickly over to get my books. The cold silence in the room was interrupted by his soft, warm, questioning words: "You'll keep this between us, won't you?"

    Still not making eye contact with him, I lowered my head, made my way toward the door, and said, "Of course I will."

    I left the classroom and headed outside. As I walked to the bus stop, I gazed up at the godly sky and clouds, searching for answers. My mind was racing in all directions, trying to make sense of what happened back there. I thought back to Mr. Benedetto and attempted to compare the two. But this was different. Very different. With Mr. Benedetto, I was frightened; but with Mr. Kurk, I felt oddly important, as if I were the chosen one, the prized student—or more like the student who got the prize. I didn't like what Mr. Kurk had done, yet I didn't hate it, either. My emotions were running amok.

On the bus ride home, my thoughts stayed on Mr. Kurk. I was surprised he took the chance of having sex with me in his classroom on the floor in my high school. Now that was one crazy fucking thought if I'd ever had one. I wondered if he'd at least locked the classroom door first, but then I realized I didn't unlock it when I left. What would have happened if someone walked in? Would he have been fired? Would I have been expelled? These thoughts sat in my gut as if I had swallowed a rock.

Several weeks went by, and Mr. Kurk had not approached me again. I was out of sorts and emotionally numb. I wondered why he cooled off and pondered if it was something I had said or done. I become tormented, almost obsessed with the possibility of rejection, until one day, when I stayed to help clean up, he asked if I wanted to see his art studio off-campus. I jumped at the chance. *Thank goodness*, I thought. *It wasn't me, after all.* It felt as if a lead weight had been lifted off my shoulders.

"You can come with me in my car," he said.

"All right, but after, can you drop me off at the bus? I have to be home by six at the latest."

"Not a problem at all." His voice was upbeat and positive. "After you," he said, motioning his hand toward the door.

He followed me, but by the time we reached the parking lot, he had taken the lead. He hummed in a cheerful tone as he swung his arms to match his long strides. I could barely keep up. I noticed how relaxed he appeared, as if this was an everyday trip with a student to his studio. I was far from comfortable, and to ease my excitement, I let myself get lost in mimicking his walk as I stared at his pants that were drooping at his nonexistent buttocks and at least four inches too long. We finally arrived at his car, which was at the farthest possible point of the employee parking lot.

On the way to the studio, Mr. Kurk continued to hum. *He's such a cheerful guy.* Oddly enough, he didn't say a word the entire ride to his art studio, which wasn't far from the school. When we drove up to the studio, it looked no different than a house from the outside.

"Is this your studio?" I asked, sounding surprised. I couldn't help but admire the beautiful flower beds and colorful pinwheels that decorated the garden. This looked more like a place that would be occupied by a woman rather than a man, or maybe a woman was responsible for placing those pretty pinwheels.

"This is my art studio. It was originally a house, but the owners converted it to a business."

I was immediately captivated by its charm. There were easels standing in various places. On them were finished paintings, and some still in progress. The walls were covered with canvases. I studied one of them that was bigger than life. When I walked closer to it, it looked like nothing more than a chaotic array of small dots in oil or acrylic. The colors were mostly brown, tan, and black in the center with dots in graffiti-like colors around the sides. There were thousands of dots on this massive canvas. Nothing was redeeming about this painting. I couldn't make out what it was, and I wondered if this was an art form I didn't know, not that I knew them all.

"I see you are looking quite perplexed by that painting. Walk backward and let me know what you see," Mr. Kurk said.

I backed up slowly. With each step I took, a face started to come into focus. When I was at least ten feet from it, the portrait was prominent and resembled a familiar face.

"Who is that?" I asked.

"That's Marlon Brando, the actor. He's one of my favorite actors, which made creating this large version even more fun and exciting."

"Aha! I thought so. It's so cool that you can't tell who it is when you're close to it." I stood there for several minutes, mesmerized by its enormity.

"It's not as easy to produce a large portrait such as this one, which comes into view when at a certain vantage point. The painting is done with a technique called pointillism, which was pioneered by Georges Seurat and Paul Seurat in Paris in the mid-1800s. Unlike Impressionism, which is based on subjective responses of individual artists, pointillism uses a more scientific approach. But, let's leave it at that. I don't want to give you all the details. I might add this topic to the class curriculum as a special assignment. Crazy as it may seem, I even know the number of dots on that canvas."

My eyes widened, and my brow furrowed as I waved my head in disbelief. "That's far out, Mr. Kurk. I mean, both teaching us and knowing the number of dots. Hey, you should have a class challenge where everyone has to guess the number of dots."

"Clever idea. Sounds like a fun *extra point* activity."

I let my gaze move away from Brando and continued to eye the rest of the room eagerly. I spotted a beautiful bay window and window seat in the center of an outer wall. It looked cozy and welcoming as the sunlight drenched the delicate floral pattern on the padded seat cover.

"I like your work, Mr. Kurk. I think I told you before, but my dad's an artist too. He paints with acrylics, oils, pastels, and charcoals. He does the most amazing wood carvings." I smiled broadly. "He is amazing. Maybe one day, you can come to my house to see his stuff and even meet him."

He walked over to a painting of a lady and asked, "Does your father paint portraits or people? Like this?"

I walked closer to admire the lady in the wide-brimmed straw hat that flopped just above her eyebrows. I stood with my hands clasped behind me, gazing at the painting, enthralled with it. The sundress she wore had large, expansive flowers in yellows, browns, greens, and oranges. The details of the bow, cinched at her waist, were so lifelike.

"This is very nice, Mr. Kurk." My voice was so low; I wasn't sure he heard me. "Is this an impressionistic painting?"

"Why, thank you, Debbie, and yes, that is impressionism. You've certainly been paying attention in class."

I walked around the studio and stopped at each painting. I was in awe of anyone's ability to bring art to life. Someday, I hoped to be just like Mr. Kurk or my father. I stopped a bit longer at another painting, a man who appeared to be a bum sitting on a park bench. I carefully scanned the canvas from the top-left corner down to the bottom-right corner.

"This one might be my favorite of all," I exclaimed. "I can't believe how real the wood on the bench looks." The crevices in the man's face depicted his age. The wrinkles boring deeply into his weathered skin reminded me of well-worn leather. And . . . his heavy, downcast eyes portrayed such sadness. "How in the world did you capture that look?"

"With a lot of training and practice."

"Mr. Kurk, how long does it take to become a great artist?"

"Many, many years. I received a degree in art at the University of New Haven, and after that, I apprenticed with a well-established artist who took me under his wing. But it was a long and arduous process and lots of mistakes along the way. You cannot even imagine how many times I had to wipe the canvas clean and start over again. Mistake after mistake after mistake. But each time I'd start over again, I got closer to achieving what I set out to accomplish."

I thought of all those knitted scarfs I had started and torn out because of one little mistake. It wasn't much different than Mr. Kurk wiping his canvas clean. I liked the idea of being able to unravel or wipe away a mistake. It would be awesome if people could wipe away or undo their mistakes, and then I shuttered at the thought of that dumb kid who tried to ride her brother's bike.

"I would love to be this good someday." I placed my clenched fist over my mouth, contemplating all that Mr. Kurk had said, and then he said, "You can be if you set your mind to it."

His words resonated with me, and I thought of Azzie. As far back as I can remember, she told me that repeatedly.

"Why are you teaching instead of painting full time?" I asked.

"Artists don't make a lot of money unless you are fortunate enough to be a Picasso, Rembrandt, or other famous painter. I know my work is good, but I'm not at that caliber. And I do show my work at an occasional art festival, but selling a painting or two does not pay the bills, so I decided I'd spread my love for art while making money at the same time."

Mr. Kurk walked closer to me. He stopped a bit too close for comfort. I took a step backward, nearly tripping over my own feet. "I'm sorry, I didn't mean to startle you," he chuckled. Then, he stretched his arms out, placed his hands on my shoulder, looked me square in the face, and said, "What would you say if I told you I'd like to paint you? Your beauty impresses me, and I think you will do justice to the canvas."

My jaw dropped open, and my eyes widened at the same time. "Uh . . . really? Me? You want to paint *me*?"

"Yes, really, you." And then came the words I never thought I'd hear: "As a matter of fact, I'd love to do a nude of you."

"I'm not sure about a nude painting," I said shyly and in a giddy sort of way. "You mean butt naked?"

"Artists paint nude portraits all the time. Come here. Let me show you a book I have."

I followed Mr. Kurk to a bookshelf filled with all kinds of art books. I noticed names like Monet, Picasso, and Dalí—most of whom I'd heard of over the years. Mr. Kurk pulled down a book called *Famous Nudes*. He opened to one of the pages and said, "Take a look at this. This painting was completed in 1586 by a man named Adam van Noort."

"Wooow . . ." The word slowly made its way out of my mouth. I stared at the painting of a lady on a horse. The name under the painting was "Lady Godiva." The woman on the horse had both legs straddled over one side. She had a swollen belly, thick thighs, and full breasts. *My mother should see her. She'd have her signed up for Weight Watchers for sure.* Her wavy hair was pulled over one shoulder and flowed down and partially over one breast, landing on top of her thigh. The horse was quite beautiful as well, and I noticed the horse's hair matched Lady Godiva's so perfectly.

"This is a very famous painting," he said as he closed the book and placed it back on the shelf. "So, what do you say? Shall we do this? I promise to keep this between the two of us."

"Oh . . . I guess I can do that." If Lady Godiva could do it, then I surely can. Besides, he's a teacher—my teacher—and a professional painter, after all.

He motioned me to a makeshift dressing room on a movable stand. "Go ahead and get undressed. There's a towel in there so you don't get cold walking around. Take a seat on the window seat over there, and I'll come over to position you for the painting."

With my hands clenched to the towel, I exited the dressing room. I strolled toward the window seat as my thoughts stirred up strange and confusing feelings. I caught a glimpse of a clock on a nearby wall and wondered how long this ordeal would take. I reached the window and sat down. I continued to clench at the towel and crossed my feet at my ankles. I'd wished he could paint me just like this.

Mr. Kurk approached me. His next words would seal the deal. "Give me the towel, Debbie." I removed it awkwardly, gazing up at the ceiling. When I let go of the towel, my fingers were stiff and my hands were clammy. Hoping Mr. Kurk wouldn't see, I dried them on the window seat cushion. "Lie partly on your side with one knee bent halfway over the other." He helped position my body to his liking and lifted my hands above my head. He backed up from me and scanned every inch of my body, returned to me, grabbed my back with both hands, and tilted me forward some. "There we go. Perfect, just perfect," he said, genuinely delighted. He stood before me scanning every inch of my body

It was awkward, to say the least, being naked in front of my art teacher; yet I was pleased he thought I was impressive enough to paint. As I began to feel a little more at ease, a sudden chill in the room caused my nipples to harden. I wanted to hide them. I felt so exposed and vulnerable. I gazed around the room to see if there was something, anything, on which I could focus. I needed to get my mind off all that had been peeled away, but there was nothing that helped. Then, I thought of Lady Godiva, and in my mind, I pretended I was her, pretended that I was important.

I focused back on Mr. Kurk, who was busy at the table next to an easel with a blank canvas. On the table sat a large, round paint palette. He mixed several colors, used several different sized brushes, and started painting stroke by stroke. I came alive on the canvas, one brush change, and one-color change after another. When he was what looked like halfway done, he announced it would be better to finish the next time because the sun had waned.

I got up from the window seat and walked toward the dressing room with the towel wrapped around me. Mr. Kurk met me halfway and then took my face into his hands. "My beautiful Debbie, I want to make love to you." I froze in the silence of his words, mesmerized by the look in his eyes. It was as if he were in a trance. I wanted him to take me—take all of me at that moment. I wanted him to quench the thirst I had for love and take the whole of me that longed for attention. He stripped before me, his body covered in a forest of thick, dark hair. He loosened my towel and let it drop to the floor. Methodically but desperately, he took me, piece by piece, as if he were creating one of his masterpieces.

When we were done, I was left with wanting more of something I knew could not be right. *Mr. Kurk, is this what you call art?*

~ ~ ~

A week later, Mr. Kurk invited me back to his studio to continue painting me. I was surprised to see that he had added more finishing touches. I got undressed and resumed my place on the window seat and positioned myself as before. Again, with each stroke he painted, I watched as he painted my nude body, until an hour later, he was finished. I wrapped the towel around me and approached the canvas. I was mesmerized by its beauty—my beauty—as it sat on the easel. The setting sun cast a shadow on the strong yet seraphic features of my face. The hair flowed loosely and delicately along my youthful breasts; the nipples peeked out from beneath.

"Do you like it?" he asked, proudly swaying his shoulders around it.

"Like it? I love it!" I said gleefully. "It's perfect."

I stared at this painting until suddenly my heart quickened and sat heavy inside my chest like a ton of bricks. I realized that I wanted to be all that the picture represented: a strong, confident, and beautiful woman. The soft curves of her hips were perfectly balanced as they flowed into legs that went on forever. There was a strong, confident young girl staring back at me. In silence, she spoke to me through the depth of her eyes. She was so full of life.

"I will keep it safe and close to my heart always," Mr. Kurk said as he approached me and placed a hand on my bare shoulder.

At that moment, it felt like my feet were glued to the floor. Every muscle in my body froze. After his advances in the classroom, I wasn't surprised by his touch. I expected it. I wanted it, yet I didn't. Did the girl in the painting want this or need this?

Now, as I watched my movie play out in some beautiful love story, he turned me toward him, dropped the robe from my body once again, and lowered me to the floor until we were entwined. I was with my knight in shining armor as we rode off into the sunset until finally I collapsed on top of Mr. Kurk while the beat of my heart tried to catch up with my breaths. I looked at his face, his age awkwardly reminding me that he could be my father.

I rolled off him and nestled on top of his left arm that wrapped around my chest. I noticed his hairy knuckles, and as if it were meant to be, a fortuitous event, or as said in Yiddish, *bashert*, I noticed a shiny gold wedding ring on his finger. I swallowed hard, but my mouth was parched. *What the fuck?* I never saw a wedding ring on his finger before. Never! I would have noticed it. I couldn't possibly have missed that. And then a chill ran up my spine and I thought, *H . . . has . . . a . . . wife! Christ!* My body became ramrod straight. I wanted the remorse to be chiseled away from what he'd done to her—for what *I'd* done to her. I tried to remove the constraints that bound us together and quickly escape. The last time we were together, I wanted more, but this time I couldn't wait to get the hell out of there. I got up abruptly.

"You're married?" I took in a deep breath, and upon exhale, my voice escalated with each word. "What the fuck? Really? How could you?" I felt all the blood drain from my face, and I struggled to hold back the tears. I slapped the top of my head with both hands, closed my eyes, and stretched out my jaw as if I were getting one of those impressions I hated dearly in my father's office.

"Debbie, please. Let me explain. My wife and I haven't been happy for years. We've agreed to stay together for the kids. I don't love her anymore."

"Happy or not happy in your marriage, I'll never forgive myself for this." I turned away and stomped my feet toward the dressing room. The tears trickled down my cheeks. I didn't want to cry in front of my teacher, but by now, he was no longer my teacher. He was a fraud, a phony, a putz. *I have to get the hell away from this slimy, slithering snake.* I could barely get dressed because my hands shook so violently and my body twitched in uncontrollable spasms.

Thank God it was close to dinner hour and time for Mr. Kurk to drop me off at the bus stop. As we walked out the door, my head hanging low, I thought, *There I go again, another piece of me chipped away. Another piece unraveled. And unlike one of my knitted pieces, this mistake would remain.*

I wasn't looking forward to going to art class anymore. As if leaving a piece of me back in his art studio wasn't punishment enough, I had lost my joy for art and had thought it might be gone forever. And although I longed for that creative piece of me to reawaken again, it would not for many, many years.

Chapter 11

"Here, have another hit." I nearly choked on the ginormous toke I sucked into my lungs. The plume of smoke nearly blinded my vision as I drove down Fountain Street. I had picked up Audrey, and we were on our way to cruise the streets of New Haven. It was just plain ole fun getting high, feeling no pain, and talking about cute boys.

"Wow," Audrey said through her laugh. "I'm about done. I'm super stoned. This is really good stuff."

"I know, right? My brother has some awesome connections, and the price is right. He never charges me for the stuff." I winked. "Lucky me."

"So sad about Jim Morrison," Audrey said as she bellowed out the lyrics to "Riders on the Storm," which I had cranked up to an obnoxious tone on the radio. Morrison had died a few weeks back, joining Joplin and Hendrix who also died of overdoses. I didn't understand much about overdosing; however, I knew my parents were concerned about Gary's drug addiction.

Whenever I thought of Gary, my heart sat heavy in my chest. It was as if the life was being squeezed out of me. Sadness would fill me up until I was drowning in sorrow, and besides, I was stoned, which didn't help. It made everything feel ten times worse, or better than it was. I had a special connection with Gary that was, and still is, hard to explain. The love I had for him made me hurt, because when he hurt, I hurt. And I genuinely believe that most of the time the pain of who he had become kept him trapped in a world of drugs, theft, and inflicting pain on others. I watched my brother—a bright, talented musician—fall prey to bad dudes.

Gary's troubles started when he was twelve years old, but who he'd become began shortly after birth when the doctor told my parents he was born with a heart murmur. From what I was told over the years, the conversation went something like this:

"Mollye and Artie, your son was born with a heart murmur. He will probably live a long life without any complications, but when a heart murmur is congenital, it can mean that a more serious heart condition may develop in the future."

"And what exactly is a heart murmur, Doc? Because, to me, 'serious' doesn't correlate to 'without complications.' Do we have to do anything about this? Do we have to treat him any differently?" my mother asked, her tone a cross between fear and confusion. She took a seat on a chair in the room, slumped her torso over her thighs, and leaned her chin on one elbow with her eyes directed at the doctor, waiting to hear more.

He continued: "A normal heart rhythm sounds like a *lubb-dupp* sound. When a heart murmur is present, you can hear a whooshing or swishing sound. The only thing I would suggest is not to let him play in any active or strenuous sports, such as football, basketball, and so on. You don't want anything to elevate his heart rate since a congenital heart murmur can be related to an underlying condition, such as a heart valve defect."

"Well, that's a lot to absorb, Doc." My father had chimed in. "So just to be sure: He can live a normal life except for strenuous activities?"

"Yep, that is correct."

From that point forward, my parents treated Gary like he was a broken boy. He wasn't allowed to participate in any activities, strenuous or otherwise. His treatment as the broken boy turned out to be what he became both literally and figuratively. As Gary neared his preteen years, my parents' protection over him had turned my brother into a shy, introverted boy. He didn't make friends easily, mainly because he didn't partake in any after-school activities.

The one true passion my brother had was music. On any given day, if he was not in his room, he was acting as a disc jockey in our den, pounding away at the piano, or strumming his guitar. Music to Gary was a welcomed respite from the tumultuous encounters with Mommy Dearest.

The den was small, to say the least—the wood-paneled room was approximately six feet by ten feet, situated just off our formal dining room. Along the back wall to one side were shelves lined with novels and Britannica encyclopedias. To the left were shelves lined with albums and records, 33s, 45s, and 78s. The numbers represented different speeds based on how many revolutions the disc made per minute. Gary's Harman Kardon turntable and Advent speakers sat on the bottom shelf. In the middle of the far wall between the shelves was a free-standing television set.

I have such sweet memories of Gary as he stood by his equipment, with a big smile on his face, when he would say, "What's your request? Will it be the Supremes or Earth, Wind & Fire? Or are you in the mood for some Streisand, James Taylor, or Tower of Power? Maybe some oldies but goodies?" I'd respond with my request, and we'd sing along to the music.

If we weren't in the den, we'd be gathered around Gary at the piano or his guitar while he'd ask for our requests. Once again, we'd sing along with him. He was a beautiful singer and so talented; he taught himself the musical score to just about any song. A favorite pastime of his was when my father would take him to Cutler's Record Shop located in downtown New Haven. His dream was to be a great musician, but if my mother had her way, that would never happen—and she always got her way. According to my mother, Gary was much better off becoming a doctor or a lawyer, a more respectable profession for a Jewish man. Gary wanted nothing to do with either of those careers.

Without sports as a deviation, and being discouraged that he could not follow his musical passion, Gary had turned to pot and was already smoking it by the time he turned twelve years old. Weed became a way for him to be noticed, to become part of the "in crowd," but unfortunately, he became a part of the "wrong crowd."

One day at school, when he was twelve, a group of older, pot-smoking, smart-ass kids approached him. They needed money to buy weed, so they conjured up a plan to get him to sell fake tickets to a concert. And he did precisely that. It worked, but the gig was up when a parent investigated and found out there was no such concert. The parent reported it to the school principal, and shortly after that, Gary was expelled from school along with the others involved.

From that day forward, Gary was sent to a private boarding school where his troubles followed him. He was caught smoking pot in the dorms and was expelled there too. His life from that point on was downhill. He became tangled up in a life of drugs, stealing from others and hurting them along the way. His drug addiction saturated his life in deep and dark ways. Both drugs and theft landed him in jail more than once. At one point, he was even on the run. After hitting rock bottom and barely escaping death during most of his adult lifetime, Gary eventually, through his faith in God and with the help of a wonderful woman, became a recovered addict. But recovery would be fleeting, as time and time again he'd succumb to his addiction. As for the heart murmur, Gary's congenital heart disease led to his first open-heart surgery at age forty-four to replace a failed aorta valve, and a subsequent surgery years later to repair additional damage.

Still deep in thought about Gary, I jolted out of my trance when Audrey turned down the radio and asked, "Hey, tell me about Jeffrey! Are you guys an item? I can tell whenever I see you two together, he is head over heels, crazy, and goo-goo-eyed over you. I mean, it is so obvious, Deb."

Trying to get my head away from Gary so I didn't accidentally say something like, "Oh, yeah, he just got expelled from Cheshire Academy," I said, "You mean Jeff?" I looked over to see Audrey nod in affirmation. "He sure is, and I'm crazy about him. He's probably the nicest guy I've ever met. I can tell because he doesn't have only one thing on his mind . . . if you know what I'm getting at."

Audrey let out a loud, guttural laugh. "You mean S-E-X? Well, I wouldn't know about that stuff because I'm still hoping to have a boyfriend one day."

I felt terrible for Audrey. Having been sick for most of her life, spending a lot of time in hospitals, and then at home recovering, she was socially behind most of us girls. And worst of all was her homeliness. The large doses of prednisone she had to be on for her regional ileitis had stunted her growth. At age sixteen, she had the figure of a boy. What little hair she had was parted in places that gave glimpses of her scalp. She was well under five feet tall, and her chest was as flat as a board. The only curves visible on her body were on her small delicate fingers.

"Yes," I giggled back at her. "Sex is exactly what I mean."

My thoughts, as stoned as I was, wandered back to Jeffrey Rosen, my new boyfriend. He was such a stand-up kind of guy, the kind I referred to as a *mensch*, the Yiddish word for "a person of integrity and honor." According to Leo Rosten, author of *The Joys of Yiddish*, a *mensch* is someone to admire and emulate, someone of noble character. Jeffrey embodied all of this and more. Not only was he kind and generous to me, but he was the same way to anyone he considered a friend. I was so lucky to have a boyfriend like him, and although I was crazy about him, I knew he was way crazier about me.

"So, what else do you want to know about Jeff? Just ask, and I shall tell." I turned up the volume on the radio a notch to hear Stevie Wonder's new release, "If You Really Love Me." I swayed to the music, still blitzed from the weed. Unlike Stevie wondering if his girl loved him, I didn't have to wonder whether Jeffrey loved me.

I knew hands down he did, and that made me feel warm inside.

"Well, let me see. Do you think you'll marry him?" Audrey squealed in a high-pitched voice. She turned toward me, eyes plastered on my face, and all ears for my response.

"I think so. He's the whole package. He's handsome and smart too. I'm grateful he helps me with my English papers. He's taught me so much. And he loves kids, so he'll make a great dad. You should see him with my nieces and nephew."

"Sweet. I should be so lucky," Audrey said. I could detect a slight sadness in her tone. Audrey desperately wanted a boyfriend. Having been so sick most of her life caused her to be extremely shy and awkward around boys.

I tried cheering her on, hoping to encourage her. "Come on, Audrey, try being a little more outgoing when we are at the next party. You are so nice and very cute." I knew she didn't believe me one bit, at least about the very cute part. Besides being below average in stature and looks, she had little confidence in ever having a boyfriend. By the time she would succumb to her illness from an overdose of pain medications, Audrey would never experience having a boyfriend.

"Next question, please," I said as I went to grab the joint sitting in my ashtray. It wasn't but a few seconds that I took my eyes off the road—or at least that's what it felt like—when I heard a loud crash that sounded like something had exploded. We had been hit, broadsided. The car spun out of control until it came to a stop on the large grassy median that divided the four lanes running east and west on Edgewood Avenue—a main artery in the city.

It all happened so fast. I was dazed and my head throbbed. I looked over at Audrey, who had ended up on the floor in front of her seat.

"Are you okay?" I yelled frantically.

"Yeah, I think so." She rubbed her head. "Can you help me up?"

I grabbed her hand and helped her into her seat.

"Are you okay?" she asked, wincing.

"I am, with the exception that my head feels like it's going to explode. I must have hit the windshield. You don't sound so good."

"I think I'm just bruised, but I do hurt pretty bad." Audrey bent her head back against the seat and placed her hands on her rib cage. I did not like the sound of her moans.

In the distance, I could hear sirens. I wasn't sure if it was a police car or an ambulance. Then, I remembered that we were smoking pot. I grabbed the joint from the ashtray and hid it in my purse. The last thing I needed just two weeks to the day after getting my license was to get arrested. And then I thought about Laurie's car. She was kind enough to let me borrow her Ford Fairlane, and I had just totaled it. *Crap, crap, crap. I'm in deep trouble now.*

Before I knew it, a police car and an ambulance pulled up next to us on the grass. An officer came over, and after he yanked on the door handle a few times, he was able to pry my door open.

"Are you guys okay?" His voice was concerned. He knelt down next to me, his eyes moving from me to Audrey and back. "Okay, listen to me. Neither of you move. The EMS practitioners are getting their stretchers ready. You both have to go to the hospital to get checked out."

On the way to the hospital, I thought about Laurie. I prayed she would forgive my stupid, dumbass mistake. Thankfully, she did. Then I thought about the long process it had taken to get my license. Six months before I turned sixteen, my mother started teaching me to drive in a parking lot. At the time, underage drivers could be instructed by a licensed driver during certain hours of the day. Eventually, she let me drive around the neighborhood, and a few weeks before my sixteenth birthday, we picked up a study manual from the Bureau of Motor Vehicles so I could prepare for the multiple handwritten tests. I had passed with flying colors, and my three-point turn was spot-on. I was ready for the big road, or at least I thought I was. Now I realized there was no chapter in the manual entitled "Learn How to Drive Stoned." I chuckled at that thought, which reminded me of the headache still looming.

~ ~ ~

Audrey and I were both lucky girls that day. We were checked in and out of the hospital on the same day with just a few scratches and bruises. Based on the pictures I saw later in the police report, one or both of us should not have survived the crash. Although seat belts were being manufactured in the early 1960s, no law required them until the mid-1980s, and airbags were not born yet for the passenger car.

I managed to get through the rest of that eleventh-grade year without crashing another vehicle. Although my sister had forgiven me for totaling her Ford Fairlane, I never asked to borrow her car again—nor did she offer it to me.

From time to time, the memory of that day would pay me a haunting visit. I'd shake my head from side to side and realize just how lucky I had been. My judgment, motor coordination, and reaction time had been altered by my choice to get high while I was driving. Before the accident, I never thought about the consequences of driving stoned. But after . . . I realized that I had a blatant disregard for my life and Audrey's. I could have died that day—or worse than my dying, I could have killed Audrey. It turned my stomach when I realized how much could have gone wrong. An arrest for possession of marijuana. Jail time for vehicular manslaughter. My life could have been ruined. Down the drain. Kaput.

Yet God had come through for me just as he had done once before.

I felt indebted to Laurie after totaling her car, so it was no surprise that during my sixteenth year, I babysat for her more than usual. Helping with the kids was my way of paying her back, although she did pay me so I'd have some of my own spending money. She and her husband, Harvey, already had two children, and their getting out was a reprieve from the daily stresses of juggling work, kids, and marriage. I never minded helping them out because I made a little extra spending money. Plus, I liked Harvey. He was a pretty laid-back, chill sort of guy. I never looked at him as an old guy because he talked to me as his equal. He was with it. Whenever I babysat, he'd spend time talking my ear off about all sorts of things. He made it easy for me to open up to him about my home life, or lack thereof. And when I got pregnant, he never judged me; in fact, he promised he would never tell a soul. And he didn't. So, other than Ivan, he was the only one who knew about the illegal abortion until afterwards when I became so deathly sick and my family took me to the hospital.

During the same year, I started working at a small kosher supermarket on Whalley Avenue called King Supermarket. All the Jews descended here to get their kosher meats and holiday specialties. I was hired as a cashier. Milton Stein, my boss, was a balding man in his late forties. He donned a long, white uniform that barely buttoned along his thick waistline. I was very excited to be working and was eager to learn. I wanted to impress my boss, so I worked extra hard, pleasing the customers by ringing up their groceries as quickly as possible.

With no barcodes, scanning devices, or digital screens back then, you had to punch a button for everything. First, you punched in the item's number, then you punched in the department number, and finally the price. After the last item was punched into the cash register, the total of the order was registered on the screen and the button marked FINAL was pushed, which caused the cashier drawer to pop out. Unlike today's registers, which calculate the amount of change, the cashiers had to count back the change out loud to the customers.

All the cashiers had individual sheets of paper protected by a plastic sleeve, all held together by one ring that slipped through a hole at the upper left-hand side. The sheets listed every type of food in the store with their corresponding item number and department number. All crackers fell under one kind of food, bread under another, apples under another, and so on. After working at King long enough, I had memorized most, if not all, of the item numbers and department numbers as well. The only thing new each week was the weekly sales flyer. The cashiers had to familiarize themselves with the sales items so they knew which items were on sale. In most cases, the customers were careful to point them out.

As my employment continued at the supermarket, I bugged Mr. Stein about teaching me new jobs in the different departments. Once he gave me that chance, I began to recognize two very dominant personality traits developing in me: the need to please and the need to excel at whatever I did. These traits weaved together stitch by stitch like one of the tightly knitted sweaters I had made. The precision of each stitch and perfection of the finished piece translated to my relationships, both professional and personal. When Mr. Stein told me there was an opening in the bakery department, I was enthralled; plus, it was a step up from being a cashier. I learned how to box cakes, cookies, hamantaschen, and all things you might find in a Jewish bakery, tying the string neatly around the boxes to secure the flaps.

I packed in as many hours as possible, including overtime when offered. The more money, the merrier, I thought, and since I didn't exactly live in the quintessential household run by Ward or June Cleaver, I was happy to be at home as little as possible.

When Mother was home, which was rare, she was screaming at one of us and using the nicknames she gave to two of my siblings: Joanne was Hitler, and Laurie was Baboon. Neither were very endearing names nor the imagined story behind the names. But Joanne was always Jo to us. I knew very little about her then. She was twelve years my senior, and I don't recall spending much time with her growing up. She had left for college when I was six years old. She met her husband during college and soon after graduating, she married and moved out of state. The relationship with her that I do remember is very different from what I had with Laurie.

I clearly remember visiting Joanne where she lived in Durham, North Carolina, when I was thirteen, a visit that would ultimately separate me from her, both physically and emotionally. The year was 1968, and I was excited to be visiting her. Although we had not been close siblings being twelve years apart, she was my big sister and, in my mind, that meant a fun trip ahead. Plus, I'd get to spend time with my nephews.

I don't recall a whole lot of detail about this trip other than my focus was a cute boy in her neighborhood. I channeled my need for attention through boys, and with no compass handed to me from either parent, this was the direction I sought out. It was as if I were a drug addict looking for her next fix.

After being introduced to this boy whom I believe was the same age as me, we quickly bonded and started hanging out. Then one day, we made plans to sit in the back seat of either his family car or my sister's family car so we could be alone. I'm not surprised I can't remember whose car it was because so much of my childhood seemed to fade into the arms of those who betrayed me. We talked, giggled, kissed, and probably even petted. I was smitten with him for no reason other than he was a boy, and he would give me attention. Our meeting was usurped by Joanne finding us in the back seat of the car. She quickly shooed him off and me into the house. I knew I was in trouble, but more than that, I was humiliated and embarrassed.

No sooner than we walked into the house, I heard, "What were you doing in that car with that boy?" She was wailing now, pacing the kitchen with my nephew hanging off her hip.

"Nothing, we were just hanging out." I could feel the tightness in my chest and pains in my stomach as if my heart and stomach were doing battle.

"Don't lie to me," she screamed. Her index finger pointed at me in a jabbing motion, much like my mother often did.

"I'm not lying, I swear. We didn't do anything wrong. He . . . he just kissed me once—that's all! What's wrong with that?" I stood there, confused. I knew I was fighting a losing battle and wanted to end the conversation before the floodgates opened. I was already humiliated, embarrassed, and defeated.

"It is wrong. You are way too young to be kissing boys. Don't let me find out that you sneaked around again with that boy. I'm not going to mention this to Nelson when he gets home. If I do, God knows what he might say to that boy. Consider yourself lucky I keep this between us."

That was the last time I visited Joanne and the last time I engaged her in any conversation. Looking back, I understand that she, too, was stepping in as the mother who was missing from my life. Her role embodied a very different one than that of Laurie's. I needed to be taught right from wrong before being reprimanded about doing something I had no idea was wrong.

As children, we hope our parents have prepared us for life in a way that shows us what appropriate behavior looks like in our interpersonal relationships. Our parents present to us our first look at what is acceptable according to societal views. When a child lacks this guidance, they unconsciously pursue what is missing, making themselves vulnerable to poor choices with insurmountable and sometimes long-term emotional impairment. Joanne had just started her role as a parent with her children, so I knew her behavior with me that day had no ill intent. She was a product of the same parents and a member of the same household. What she took away from and surmised from the chaotic family we grew up in at 83 Curtis Drive was what she displayed to me that day.

As a result of the chaos in the Barnett household, any chance I had to stay away, I did. Being at home was like living in the wild among animals—only worse. Unlike a wild pack of animals, my house had no parental control, no assemblage of order, and no love. If I heard my mother yelling or screaming at one of my siblings, or chasing them around the house, I'd crank up the transistor radio to drown out the noise. I counted down the years until I would turn eighteen, anxiously awaiting my escape. Being at work gave me the respite I needed. When I walked into the King Supermarket, I'd let out a big sigh of relief. The longing to be a part of some normalcy was always calling to me and was what I needed. I was like a lost kid in an amusement park, trying to find her way back to a safe harbor—only my safe place was nowhere to be found.

When I was at work, I had come close to a feeling of belonging. I was an essential part of a team. I was a member of the King family and feeling a part of a family was just what I needed. That was . . . until six months into my employment. I was in the back room, where the time clock was kept. I grabbed my timecard and stuck it into the clock, waiting to hear the punch. When I pulled it out and placed it back in its rightful place, I turned to see Mr. Stein standing in front of me. I had no time to think, no time to react. Mr. Stein pressed me up against the wall, forcefully kissed me, and cupped my breasts in his hands.

It took all my strength to lift one leg and plunge it forward, causing him to buckle at the knee. "Whoa! Easy does it!" he responded, as if trying to pull the reins in on a horse.

"Stop! Get the fuck off me!" I yelled while my arms tried to pry him loose. He was surprised by my choice of words, but his persistence continued. His first failed attempt angered him. His face was gnarled with disgust as he once again tried to kiss me. I was helpless under his overweight body. The floodgates opened and tears spilled down my cheeks. I continued to shout, "Stop, stop! Why are you doing this?"

He finally backed off, most likely fearful that someone might hear. I was shaking in horror and disbelief at what had just happened, but with all the strength I had in me, I blurted out, "I quit!" I walked back to the bakery department, grabbed my purse, and never went back to work at King Supermarket again. I don't remember the lie I fed my mother about why I quit, but I never told her about that incident with Mr. Stein. I needed to preserve any sense of self I had. Besides, it wouldn't have mattered to her anyway, or she would have convinced me to just forget about it. Hush up, keep it a secret. She'd protect others over me, being more concerned about what others would think.

And just like that, my family at King Supermarket came to an end. I was sensing a consistent pattern developing in my social edifice. I had become a magnet, strong and mighty, drawing through my weakness the men who took advantage of me, the men who knew how to abuse their power and prey on my weakness. I had never asked for Mr. Benedetto to teach me about open marriages. I had never asked Mr. Kurk to give me art lessons consisting of his painting me nude or making love to me while cheating on his wife. Nor did I seduce Mr. Chovnik into raping me.

My fate was being sealed like a slowly unraveling mystery, scene by scene, character by character, bit by bit.

Chapter 12

The disco era was in full bloom. Discos were filled with girls in wide-legged pant suits that showed off their cleavage, while the boys showed off their chests in large, pointed collared shirts, opened nearly to their belly buttons. Both men and women were wearing platform shoes back then, and the more glitter the merrier. Bouncers at the discos were more lenient during the early seventies. If you looked old enough to get in, then you got in. If you looked young for your age . . . well, you were out of luck. I was fortunate enough at sixteen to look twenty.

Pot smokers did not decrease their use of the drug even after the passage of the 1970 Controlled Substances Act, which outlawed its use. Cleaning weed became quite a skill, from breaking up flower buds to removing seeds and stems. And rolling joints became a new art form.

With my innate artistic abilities, I became a crackerjack joint roller, spreading the marijuana evenly along the rolling paper to form the perfect specimen of a joint. My joints were indeed admired by many.

The Vietnam War was still underway, already taking the lives of over fifty thousand US troops. Antiwar protesters weren't letting up, and on May 3, 1971, a little over a month before my tenth-grade year ended, protestors calling themselves the Mayday Tribe began their three-day demonstrations in Washington aimed at shutting down the capital. Thirteen thousand of them were arrested over the three-day period.

Racial strife was still working its way through daily life, and Archie Bunker made it known on *All in the Family* that it was "okay" to air racism on public television. Racial discrimination was far from over.

I was pleased that the Carpenters, one of my favorite singing duos, had made number two on the pop singles chart with their song "Rainy Days and Mondays." It was pretty neat that I got to pass by their home in East Haven on my way to Colony Beach Club, where I spent many summer days.

I would be entering the eleventh grade after learning the "art" of a tempestuous relationship under the mentorship of Mr. Kurk and the fall of the King family. Azzie's presence at home and her protective shield had started to fall apart. The older the kids got, the less she was needed at home, the less she was with me and my brother, and the less she was there to remind me of my self-worth. After each immoral and bastardly adult male relationship I had encountered in the past three years, I found myself becoming withdrawn, a social outcast, a misfit of sorts among my peers. In my mind, I was different from the thousands of students who meandered around the school grounds. I became that perceptible "blonde shit" and "that girl" all over again, and I compared myself to every girl who walked by me: "Am I prettier? Am I thinner?"

Other than Anat and Audrey, I had few friends and Jeffrey was one of them. I was not a part of the "in crowd" or the popular girls who had dozens of friends. They hung out with the football and basketball players; they were cheerleaders. I often walked the school hallways alone. The isolation at times was unbearable until the day Maria Barros and I became friends. Maria was a beautiful, dark-complexioned Hispanic girl with large, olive-shaped eyes. She could light up any room with her huge smile. Although we had been sitting next to each other in Spanish class, we had never really spoken until now. She was gregarious yet shy, all wrapped up neatly into the perfect match for me. The magnetism in our friendship became magical, and as it grew, Maria let me know she didn't care what others said or thought of me. We became "besties."

One afternoon, when Spanish class had concluded, Maria approached me and asked if I would like to come to her house after school the next day. She lived within walking distance to the school. I told my mother a little white lie; after all, she was the creator of the white lie and because, sadly, I had no choice. Maria was not a white Jewish girl. Mommy would surely not approve. I had told her I had a project to work on but would be home by dinnertime. She was concerned with my walking to the bus stop alone, but I assured her there were lots of kids from the neighborhood to walk with me, so she agreed.

After school the next day, Maria and I walked to her home. As soon as we entered her apartment, I noticed some vast differences. In comparison, her home seemed much smaller than mine yet much warmer. Except for a few pictures hanging on the walls, the room felt very stark next to our house that had rooms filled with furniture and my father's art everywhere. Her mom approached me and immediately embraced me in a warm hug. "You must be Debbie. I'm so happy to meet you." She ushered me inside. "Please come in, sit down, and make yourself at home."

The room I entered was the only room for gathering. I remember thinking, *Do people actually live in such small homes?* The smell in the house was delightful, and I could feel my taste buds dancing, begging for a taste of whatever was cooking. I sat down, and before I pulled in my chair, Maria's mom was in the kitchen and back with a tray of homemade cookies and ice-cold milk.

"Please, please, take one, my dear. I know you must be hungry after a long day at school," she said.

"Thank you," I replied, taking a cookie and biting into it. "Wow, these are delicious, Mrs. Barros."

"I like to have cookies made for my Maria when she gets home," she said in a singsong voice. I repeated the words to myself, with a slight alteration. *"I like to have cookies made for my Debbie."*

While Maria and I ate cookies and drank milk, Mrs. Barros asked me all sorts of questions:

How many brothers and sisters did I have, their ages, my favorite subject in school, and so on. I could not believe a mother could be so interested in a stranger's life, and as odd as it seemed, it was warm and comforting.

When it was time to leave, I thanked Mrs. Barros profusely for the hospitality. Maria walked me to the bus stop, and all the while, I was envious. I witnessed something inside her home that told me something was missing from my life, something I was afraid would never be found.

Because . . . perhaps it never existed.

My friendship with Maria grew, and so did the little white lies I told so I could spend time with her after school. But I had to put a stop to them eventually. Although I knew the outcome might not be good, it was time to invite her to my house to meet my mother. I was going to be a senior the next year, and as soon as I turned eighteen, I'd be off to college, never to return to 83 Curtis Drive. *What do I have to lose, anyway?* The first night of Passover was March 29, a Wednesday night. I thought it would be a perfect time for Maria to meet my parents, and since most of my siblings would be there (and my grandparents), they'd all be the reason for my mother to be as sweet as pie. The holiday dinner was to begin at

6:00 P.M. My grandparents from both sides of the family had come early.

Seeing Grandma Cecelia, my father's mother, at the holiday dinner that evening was not surprising because I assumed she had accepted the invitation out of respect to my grandfather Gustave and my father. But if my grandma had it her way, I doubt she'd ever step foot in our house. Cecelia detested my mother and the family from which she came. My understanding was that she thought my mother's social class was not good enough for my father. I can still recall the day they had an altercation that resulted in my mother leaving rather abruptly

~ ~ ~

My mother, Kenny, and I walked into my grandmother's very modest two-bedroom apartment on Blake Street in New Haven, where she had moved after my grandfather had passed away. Her front door was ajar, and when we rang the bell, we could hear my grandmother yell for us to come in. As soon as we entered the apartment, the same stale, unpleasant odor that greeted us each time made my nose twitch. Passing by a tiny kitchen, we made our way into the living room, where we found my grandmother sitting in her usual drab light-yellow vinyl chair. The blinds were drawn, and the only light came from a half-burned-out bulb flickering from a lamp next to her. "Come here and give your Grandma a kiss," she said.

I walked over to her where I reluctantly kissed her on the lips, my brother following suit. The smell of her skin and breath seemed to match the stale odor that greeted us upon arrival. I had to hold my breath when I kissed her. I wanted to gag. I wondered if the smell on her skin and breath were a part of being old; yet my other grandmother, my mother's mother, always smelled so sweet.

"How are you, Silch?" my mother asked. Silch was my grandmother's Yiddish name. Her birth name was Cecelia, yet I don't remember referring to her as anything but Grandma Silch. My mother took a seat on the sofa draped with an afghan made of smaller individual crocheted squares.

Silch mumbled, "I'm okay, same as usual. I sit here alone all day. No one visits. You know, it would be nice if I saw the kids more often, but you're too busy with your friends to bring them over. Maybe if you stayed home more, I could see my grandchildren more."

"Silch, I don't think it is any of your business whether I'm home or not."

"It *is* my business. You are married to my son." My grandmother straightened up in her chair and leaned forward. She meant business.

Kenny and I were sitting on the carpet and watching the two of them. We both looked at each other cockeyed, and Kenny gave me a broad smile. I could tell he was about ready to crack up. He must have thought the banter between them was funny. I found it quite awkward.

My mother wasn't about to listen to any more from my grandmother. She got up abruptly from her chair and motioned Kenny and me out the door.

It was during that visit that it became apparent to me why my grandmother referred to my mother as "zi," the Yiddish word for "she." She despised my mother so much that she wouldn't even call her by her name. My understanding is that my grandmother never thought my mother was good enough for my father, so there was no love lost from the beginning of their relationship. To be fair to my mother, Cecelia was an unpleasant woman. The scowl usually worn on her face screamed an undeniable dislike for those in her presence. Her frigid demeanor created a barrier so dense that a hello kiss froze to her aging skin, an impenetrable sign that she didn't want or need your love. The only redeeming thing I remember about Grandma Cecelia is the roasted eggplant relish she made.

My grandfather Gustave, Silch's husband, referred to as Grandpa Gus, was just the opposite in personality, and their differences were as vast as those of my Grandpa Nate and Grandma Rose—only, in this case, Grandpa Gus was the more docile of the two. He was a soft-spoken, warm, positive person whose ability to speak was robbed by laryngeal cancer from smoking. I can still remember my fascination with the external transcervical device that he held against his neck to speak. The device resembled an electric razor, which, when operated, caused the muscles and mucosa of the oropharyngeal space to vibrate. It created a robotic sound, a potentially frightening proposition for a young child unless under the positive influence of Grandpa Gus, who made the experience seem pretty cool. He died years before my grandmother did; I was eleven years old.

~ ~ ~

The doorbell rang. My friend Maria had arrived. I walked her into the living room where everyone was gathered and introduced her. No one else noticed, but my mother's piercing looks nearly caused her eyeballs to fly right out of her head. She coldly said nothing more than, "Hi."

I was embarrassed, my cheeks were on fire, and the sweat beaded on my forehead. I became paralyzed by my mother's rudeness and wanted to apologize for her shameful behavior. I thought back to my visit to Maria's home and couldn't believe how completely different our two mothers were. I couldn't look Maria in the eyes, so I awkwardly ignored her until a short while later when Azzie announced it was time for dinner.

Dinner was the typical conservative Jewish Seder led by my Grandpa Nate. The table was dressed elegantly with my parents' most beautiful linens and dinnerware along with an assortment of traditional Jewish foods such as gefilte fish, kasha varnishkes, kugel, potato latkes, challah, and a Seder plate filled with six items all having significance in Jewish history. Of course, Passover would not be complete without the traditional Manischewitz Jewish wine.

Maria sat with her eyes and ears attentive to the ceremony and the Hebrew words spoken by my grandpa. She'd been working at a Jewish assisted living facility and knew quite a few Jewish customs and traditions; she was eager to learn more. On the other hand, I waited anxiously for the long and arduous ceremony to be over so the little ones could get to the best part: finding the afikomen.

Finding the afikomen is a Jewish tradition in which you break the middle matzoh into two uneven parts, concealing the larger piece in a linen napkin and returning the smaller piece to its rightful place. After the Seder, in a sort of hide-and-seek game, the larger section is then hidden for the younger children to find. The eye on the prize meant a reward: either a piece of candy or money. However, it has been said the real meaning of setting this piece of matzoh aside is a reminder to the poor to save something for their next meal. Another interpretation is a reminder that, in life, there is always more to discover. My nieces and nephews partook in the game that evening and even my fourteen-year-old brother. Dinner concluded at 8:00 P.M., and Maria and I hung out in my room until her father picked her up at 8:30 P.M. Once she—and everyone else—left, I heard my mother yell for me to come downstairs. She was already waiting for me at the bottom of the staircase. "I don't think you should be hanging around colored people," she blurted out.

"What!" I screamed. "She is not colored. She is Hispanic! And what difference does it make, anyway?"

"She may be Hispanic, but she has dark skin, and that makes her colored. I do not think it's a good idea to bring her around here. Period. The end."

"God, I hate you," I said, tears welling up in my eyes. I turned away from her and ran fast up the staircase. Like an impala, I leaped over the steps, skipping every other rung until I was gasping for air and had finally reached the top. I trudged to my room, my legs like jelly, desperately trying to collapse under me. I shut my door and flopped atop my bed. I was devastated. *What just happened?* I thought, tears running down my face and soaking my shirt. *Why did that happen? I hate her. I hate her. I hate her. She is ruining my life. First Donna and now Maria. How could she do this to me?*

I got up to get dressed for bed, the mucus from my nose still running into my mouth, the salt from my tears stinging my skin.

I heard Azzie's soft voice. "Baby Girl? Can I come in?"

"Yeah, sure." I didn't even bother hiding my teary face.

Azzie came in and sat on the edge of my bed. She laid her hand gently on my arm.

"By now, you ought to be used to your mama. I know this is hard on you. Your heart don't see color, and that's a beautiful thing. Ya hear? That's a beautiful thing, Baby Girl. I know, and you know, your mama doesn't know any better. I'm telling you, stay true to yourself, and that beautiful heart of yours will make you a beautiful life."

I didn't say a single word, but my silence spoke volumes as I looked into Azzie's eyes and smiled through my tears.

I never told Maria about this. It would be just another Barnett household secret I would add to my broken-heart arsenal. From that day on, I only went to Maria's home. I used excuses for not having her over or suggested we hang out downtown after school. In my heart, though, I knew she knew the truth.

Maria gave more to me in our short friendship than so many others had. In her unique way, she taught me just as Azzie had that there is goodness in everyone, no matter their background, color, or ethnicity. I adored her. Maria showed me that a house is not a home without the doors being open to all and welcoming arms waiting for you.

Chapter 13

It all came back to me, like a tsunami flooding my mind with diseased memories. I had locked this piece of the story—my story—away in a safe box for years. But those memories still haunted me. It wasn't until I read yet another young girl's story of abuse by a family member that I knew I had to tell the truth. The truth could be heard in those young girl's cries just as they had been in mine. The truth made me sick, and I wanted to leave those days behind. I wished them away, vanished from my mind like a science-fiction mind-manipulating movie, or wiped out like the clean slate of a chalkboard. If telling my story could help heal me or just one more person, then I would be happy with my decision to tell mine.

~ ~ ~

My sophomore year of high school was underway, and during that year, I spent a great deal of time at Laurie's to help her with the kids and to babysit. I loved kids, especially my nieces and nephew. And I loved babysitting, so it was a win-win for both of us. I did everything with and for the kids, taking them out for food, shopping, bathing, feeding, playing with them, as I'd always done with past babysitting jobs; I treated the kids as if they were my own. The piece of me that had yearned to be a mother, the kind of mother I had never had, became a strong presence in my life. It was one that I played out in my own fictitious world of babysitting.

Laurie lived in a three-story townhouse that included the main floor, an upstairs where the bedrooms were located, and a finished basement with a pull-out sofa, where I slept when I stayed over. She was married to Harvey, a nice-looking man with deep-blue eyes that stood out among his thick, dark, straight head of hair. Despite his sometimes playful and sarcastic personality that came across as feigned, he could be very charming. I enjoyed chatting with him when he could put aside his insincere quips. He went out of his way to make me feel comfortable in a buddy sort of way, and over time, I shared stories of my life, boyfriend woes, and even my unavoidable botched abortion. To this day, I'm not quite sure why I had confided in him about the abortion, but I did. He was, after all, the one I asked to phone my mother that dreadful night. Maybe it was because he had made it clear to me that he would not judge me in any way while I thought others might. My sister was more of a mother figure to me and a take-charge "someone has to be there for you and your younger brother" person. Whatever the reason for confiding in Harvey, I often wondered why he didn't protect me from that upcoming event. Why hadn't he gone to Laurie or Jeff or my mother?

Over time, my friendship with Harvey grew, and it wasn't until that night back in 1971 that our friendship headed in another direction, another dimension. I babysat for Laurie that night while she was out for an evening with friends. Harvey was also out that evening but had returned home earlier than usual. I was upstairs in their bedroom on top of their queen-size bed where I customarily watched TV so I could listen for the kids. When Harvey walked into his room, I said shockingly, "Wow, you're home early."

"I was supposed to have dinner with a friend, but he canceled on me, so here I am." There was an odd snicker in his response as if he'd said something funny. He disappeared into his master bathroom. I heard him gargle and then spit out what I assumed was mouthwash into the sink. When he returned, he asked, "What are you watching?" Again, I heard an odd snicker in his voice.

"*The Twilight Zone*, one of my favorites." I was trying to pay attention to the show but had one eye on Harvey as he took off his watch, dropping it and his wallet onto the dresser. He paced the room and cleared his throat a few times. If I didn't know any better, it appeared he was in the waiting room awaiting news of his first-born child. I wasn't sure what was going on, but something didn't feel quite right to me, and although I couldn't place my finger on it, his coming home early seemed a bit odd.

He walked over to his side of the bed and stood there motionless. I wasn't sure if he was watching me or the TV. Finally, he plopped on the bed next to me, and said, sounding out of breath, "Mind if I watch with you?"

"No, of course not," I said, but I *did* mind. His behavior from the time he returned home up until this very moment began to upset me. Nausea settled into the pit of my stomach as if I had just swallowed a lead weight. I was nervous and on edge, the sort of feeling you get when you're unprepared to take a final exam.

With *The Twilight Zone* in the background, and the one I had no idea I was about to enter, Harvey started up an idle conversation. He reiterated being my friend and reassuring me I could talk to him about anything, and then the flattery came, just like Mr. Kurk had done. "You know, Debbie, you are quite beautiful and special, and I like you. Sometimes, when I talk to you, it's hard for me to believe you're only sixteen. And besides, I feel as if you get me way more than your sister does."

Get him more than my sister does? What does that mean?

"Gee, thanks," I said, allowing his words to fall out of his mouth and onto my wounds. He and his words were there for me, both ready to soothe my already broken sixteen-year-old spirit, ready to fill the void I needed to hear: "You are worthy. You are wanted. You are good enough." The more his words massaged me, the more I longed for . . . more words. And when he made his first move on me, a kiss, it quickly foreshadowed all that led up to my need to fill the emptiness that lived inside. I was in a state of shock, yet I didn't stop him. Why? What the fuck? Without enough time to sort this out in my head, Laurie returned home, just minutes later.

Harvey quickly jumped up from the bed and straightened himself out. I did as well. I smoothed out the bed to be sure not to leave any evidence. I had converted back to Laurie's baby sister and babysitter as if nothing had happened. I heard her footsteps at the top of the staircase and then watched as she made her way toward the bedroom.

"How did it go, Deb?" she asked.

"Great as always. A bit of a hard time getting them to bed, but really, they are wonderful. I love them so much." I abruptly stood up and said, "I'm exhausted. I can hardly keep my eyes open. I'm going to head to bed."

"See you in the morning." As I was heading down the first-floor landing, I could hear their conversation.

"So how was your night with the girls?"

"Fun, it was fun. How about you? How was dinner with Ben?"

"Dinner was fine. I hadn't seen him in so long. It was great catching up."

Hmmm . . . why is he lying to her? Crap.

I continued to the basement. I wondered if everyone in this world lied. It was usual and customary business in the Barnett household, so maybe it was just the ordinary course of things. Once in the basement, I undressed and lay in bed. An army of doubt and guilt and fear had infiltrated and invaded my thoughts. I screamed those words again . . . *Why me? Why didn't I get up when he first walked into the room? I could have said no when he asked if he could watch TV with me. But I didn't . . . oh, fuck! I didn't. I didn't like what he did one bit—not one bit. I swear, God, do you hear me? Not one bit.*

I wasn't sure if I was trying to convince God or myself, but I knew what Harvey had done to me was not the "normal course of business." And as much as I tried to fall asleep, the troops were winning out and the words kept coming. *Did he plan this? Was he ever really meeting a friend for dinner? Oh, fuck, fuck, fuck! I cannot tell Laurie, no way, no how. I can't ruin her entire life. Maybe this will never happen again. Right.... this will never happen again . . . and just like a bad dream, it will all go away.* As I soothed my thoughts with these comforting words, I had finally won this war—at least for now—and slipped into the world where I could feel safe.

After that first night with Harvey, I was consumed by the thought of what had happened. I dreaded the next time Laurie might ask me to babysit. I wanted to come up with some lame excuses: "Hey, Laur, I can't sit tonight. I'm leaving in the morning. I've decided to do the Kibbutz thing" or "Hey, Laur, the headmaster at Lee High is letting me skip the rest of this year and the next three, so I'm heading off to college."

I was stuck. Period. The end. I had no choice; I would have to babysit again, but maybe—just maybe—I could come up with an excuse that might work. In the meantime, I was hoping that spending a lot of time with Jeffrey driving around and getting high, as usual, would help. It did to some extent; however, I was always preoccupied, not present a lot of the time we were together, and Jeff knew something was up. Weed, which normally relaxed me, was making me paranoid, sending me into retreats of panic and fright. As hard as I tried, I could not get it out of my mind. I started turning away the weed just to avoid the paranoia.

I always played tennis better when stoned, so one afternoon on the court, when I refused a hit on his blunt, Jeffrey asked in a concerned voice, "Hey, when do you ever refuse a hit?"

I kept my head low, refraining from eye contact.

"Look at me, please?" But I didn't dare. So he persisted. "And tell me nothing is going on. Please, I need to know. Is it something I did? Is there someone else?" His voice rose with each sentence until he was nearly screaming to get me to look at him.

"Oh, God, no, there is no one else. I'm okay. I am." I put my arm around his waist and placed my head on his chest. "It's just stuff at home, ya know. My brother and his drug addiction crap are pretty messed up. It's always chaos at home, and I think it's just starting to get to me."

"Sorry, Babe." He took my face in his hands. I was afraid he might feel the dampness from the tears I was failing at holding back. "I'm here if you need to talk. You know that, don't you?"

"I do know that."

I gave him a soft embrace and a peck on the cheek and whispered in his ear, "In the meantime, let's play tennis. I need to kick your ass again!"

"Ha ha ha," he said with a belly laugh. "I doubt it! There is no way I'm letting you whip my butt again."

"We'll just see about that." I jumped up and ran for my racket.

After I won the match four to three, Jeffrey gave me a congratulatory squeeze and muttered, "I let you have that last game."

"Yeah, sure you did," I said, celebrating and kicking up my heels.

Later that day when I was home, the phone rang. It was the phone call from Laurie I'd hoped would never come. "Hi! Are you free next Saturday night?"

"Uh . . . uh . . . my, my damn laundry is piling up. I literally just threw my last pair of underwear down the laundry shoot. I was going to spend the weekend catching up on my laundry." *Oh crapola . . . did I just say that to my sister? Maybe I should throw myself down the laundry shoot.*

"Come on, you are joshing with me, aren't you?" She let out a giggle and then continued, "You can bring your laundry here and do it."

Trying not to sound too disappointed, I forced a gleeful "Sounds great!" out of my mouth.

"I'll pick you up five thirty on Saturday, okay? You'll eat dinner with us. I'm making a pot roast, and then Harvey and I are going to the movies."

"Sure." I said it so softly I wasn't sure if she heard me, and then I heard the dial tone affirming she had. *Okay, dumbass, you could have come up with a better excuse. You're stuck now. Good luck to you and your dirty laundry too!* Then, a sigh of relief washed over me. Did I hear her say, "Harvey and I are seeing a movie"? Yes, yes, yes! It's all good, they will be together, and I will not have to be alone—with him.

Saturday had arrived, and there I was, sitting around the dinner table with Harvey, Laurie, and the two kids while Neil Diamond's album, "Touching You, Touching Me" was playing in the background. I thought about the title of that album, and a chill ran up and down my spine like a never-ending relay game.

"How do you like my new cassette deck Harvey gave me for our anniversary?"

I turned to look at it and, making sure I sounded excited for her, said, "That's awesome! Looks like top of the line." What I really wanted to say was, *What a great anniversary gift, Harvey. You must really love my sister; otherwise, why would you get her such an expensive gift? You do love her, right? You would never hurt my sister, would you?*

"Yes, it is," my sister gushed. "Harvey tells me it's one of the best out there."

After dinner, Laurie and I cleaned up, and while they got ready to go out, I bathed the kids and got them in their pajamas. The kids and I sat in the living room and watched the *Mickey Mouse Club*.

Laurie and Harvey came downstairs. "I know you kids will be sleeping when I get home, so I'll see you tomorrow," Laurie said, kissing each of them on their heads. "Love you!"

Barely taking their eyes off the TV set, as if in some trance, they waved goodbye. After being begged a thousand times, the kids talked me into watching another episode. Nestled together on the sofa, we waited until the closing theme song began, one of the best parts of the whole show. Our eyes were glued to the screen until every last word chimed out of Jimmy and the gang: "M-I-C—See you real soon!—K-E-Y—Why? Because we like you!—M-O-U-S-Eeeeee." It was hard not to love that show. I had been watching it since I was a kid too.

"Hop to it, kiddos. It's time for bed." I followed the little ones as they walked up the staircase in a slow, sleepy gait. I tucked them into their beds and kissed them good night. With a gut-wrenching "go ahead and tear my insides out" feeling, I settled myself onto Laurie and Harvey's bed, turned on the TV, and asked Scotty to "beam me up."

Laurie and Harvey came home shortly after eleven and rudely, without even asking how the movie was, I excused myself and headed down to my quarters in the basement. It wasn't more than an hour later, barely awake, I saw Harvey standing in front of me at the foot of the bed. I thought I imagined the form of him there and prayed it was all a bad dream, but then when he climbed onto the bed and on top of me, his body forcefully executing every move, my world stood still and I was back in another *Twilight Zone* episode. Instead of the real episode, "An Occurrence at Owl Creek Bridge," a story of a southern civilian who escapes his hanging at the hands of union soldiers when the rope breaks, my episode was called, "An Occurrence at Dead End Lane," a story of a young girl who could not escape the hands of her sister's husband. I was literally and figuratively trapped. My body couldn't and didn't react, and my mind desperately tried to escape . . . and it did. I pretended to be Dorothy with Toto by my side, leaving my body and slipping into another space and time among the beautiful poppies where I drifted away.

Once he left, I fell deep into a dream. Azzie and my mother were floating above me, facing me. Both yelled at me while at the same time duking it out with each other. "Have you no shame, Debbie? What were you thinking? Apparently, you weren't!" my mother belted out while waving her index finger at me.

"Leave her alone, for God's sake!" It was Azzie coming to my side. "She is a child. Maybe if you'd been around a bit more—"

My mother cut Azzie off abruptly. "Who are *you* to tell *me* what I should or shouldn't have done with *my* child? You are not her mother!"

"I may not be her mother, but I've given her more in her young life than you have."

"Stop!" I screamed. "Stop, please, just stop. I know I deserved this. I did. It's all my fault. Oh, God, I'm so sorry, please just make them stop." The blankets flew off me, and my head was thrashing on my pillow as if I had been exorcised. Then, I jumped out of the bed and spied the room for my mother and Azzie, but they were nowhere to be found. I got back into bed and flipped the tear-stained pillow over to the dry side. As hard as I tried, Toto was nowhere to be found.

~ ~ ~

The reality of the abuse was starting to take its toll on me. It had been going on for months now. Fear kept me trapped in something I didn't understand and something I didn't know how to sever. The complexity of what had happened the first, second, third, or fourth time Harvey abused me was so hard for me to wrap my head around. As much as I tried, I couldn't make sense of something that seemed so unreal. Most of the abuse was going on just a couple floors under where my sister slept peacefully in her bed. I never enjoyed his advances, but I was petrified of the outcome if I told someone. *Would they believe me, or would they blame me? Would I turn my whole sister's life upside down? Would my entire family turn their backs on me?* Continually, these questions played in my mind, like a scratch on a 45 vinyl record, looping back and forth, forth and back. If I stopped babysitting and sleeping over, my sister would assume something was wrong and I might be forced to tell her. That thought scared the crap out of me, because Laurie had been the one sister who was always there for me no matter what. I knew she would still have my back, and now it felt like I was betraying her.

Each time Harvey left, a vulnerable rawness was left behind, a cruel reminder that lingered for days, just as his beard had irritated my skin and chaffed my lips. Many nights I'd lie in bed having conversation after conversation with God: *God, why me? God, how many other girls are experiencing this right now? God, how do I get myself into these situations? God, are all men evil? God, what should I do?* I knew I had to find the strength to figure it out. I knew God would surely come through for me, because Azzie's presence, for some unknown reason, had failed me in this time of need. Was it because I had failed her? I was saddened at the thought but knew I had to be brave somehow, someway. I had to believe that even though Azzie wasn't there in the way I wanted her to be, she had defended me against my mother. That was good, but not good enough to provide me with the help I needed, so I looked to God for guidance. Although he had never spoken to me directly, I prayed and I prayed and I prayed that he would give me a sign.

As if things couldn't get worse, one evening, Harvey professed his love for me. The thought of it made me gag. Did he think he would divorce my sister, and we would get married? I never shared a word of my feelings to him. I never approved of what he was doing. Never. Never. Never. I hated every minute of the grotesque nightmare that had now turned from abuse to perverse. I needed answers, and I needed them now. I knew this had to stop. I knew I could no longer live in this hellish nightmare. I begged and pleaded to God to help me out—and He finally did. The answer He told me was there all along. The help I needed had been by my side from the beginning. I would tell Jeffrey.

Chapter 14

We made our way up through the winding one-lane road of West Rock, slowing at each switchback. West Rock, and its tunnel that separated New Haven from Hamden, was a favorite place of mine and for most teenagers to hang out, make out, and get high. The red cedar and chestnut oak trees along the cliffs were lush this time of year, so it wasn't unusual to find hikers trekking their way up the seven-mile stretch.

When we reached the top, Jeffrey and I pulled into our usual spot overlooking the city. The sky was painted in a turquoise blue, absent of all clouds, which occupied my thoughts. I was about to disclose the worst thing a girlfriend could ever tell her boyfriend. I had planned my discussion with Jeff for days, yet there I sat, feeling unrehearsed. When I mustered up enough guts, I snuggled up to Jeffrey and lay my head on his chest. I knew it would be easier if I didn't have to look him in the eyes. "Jeffrey," I said with hesitation. "I need to tell you something."

"Sure, anything." He kissed me on my forehead. "You know you can talk to me about anything."

"Okay," I said, trying to catch my breath, "but this is very hard for me to talk about, and I don't want this to ruin what we have together."

"Nothing can or will ruin this, Debbie. As long as we love each other, we can get through anything."

Hmmm, I thought. Those words sound vaguely familiar.

"Okay, here it goes." I sat up, refraining from looking him in the eye, took a deep breath, my diaphragm filling with air like an overinflated balloon, and blurted out, "You know my sister's husband? You've met him a few times, I believe, while I was babysitting."

"Yep, Harvey, of course." He nodded.

"Well, he has been sexually abusing me for months."

Jeffrey sat up, his body stiffening as if rigor mortis had set in, and his mouth opened wide enough so I could see all his silver fillings. It reminded me of the fun Kenny and I had playing with the mercury my father had carefully measured out, depending on the depth of each filling. The jellylike, slippery, and shining globs that were nearly impossible to hold between our fingers. I proceeded to tell him every detail, and when I was finished, the loudest "*What?*" I had ever heard spurted out of his mouth. It was so loud it caused my body to jerk backward against the seat.

And then I cried uncontrollably. The weight of what Harvey had done to me was finally being lifted just enough for someone to come in and steady me. His "What?" sounded like he was upset, but I was hoping it wasn't all directed at me. "I hated it, Jeffrey, every fucking minute of it, but I was stuck in a bad dream, or more like my body was stuck in quicksand, sinking deeper and deeper into something I couldn't remove myself from. I'm afraid to tell my sister. God, Jeffrey, she just found out she's pregnant with their third child!" Sobbing even harder now, I placed my face in my hands. He was silent. He didn't say a word. I could hardly believe what I just told my boyfriend. *This can't possibly be real. Does he think I was cheating on him? Is that how he sees this?*

And then Jeffrey slammed his fist on top of the dashboard and laid his head on the steering wheel. "Let me handle this. I will go and speak to her. You can't let this go on any longer, and that man cannot get away with this." I nestled my face into his chest while drying my snot on his T-shirt. "Now get a hold of yourself, okay? We will get through this because we have each other, right?" I lay there listening to the beat of his heart. My sobbing subsided when, at last, I let the air out of my chest.

Jeffrey called my sister that night, and he made a date to see her the next day. I was glad it was the weekend instead of the school week. He told me later how he handled it.

He had arrived at Laurie's house, and she had opened the door and showed him in.

"Let's sit at the kitchen table," she said. "You've got me really worried. Is Debbie okay?" She sat down, crossed her arms, and stared at my boyfriend, waiting for him to answer.

"Yes, she's fine. I mean, she's not fine, but she's not hurt." Jeffrey had a hard time at first getting it all out. "Oh, God, I mean she *is* hurt but not physically speaking."

Fidgeting, my sister stood up and sat down again, let out a huff, and said impatiently, "Just tell me, please. What's wrong?"

"Harvey has been sexually abusing Debbie for months." There. He had said it.

Apparently, Laurie stared at him for a brief moment before breathing out, "Oh my God." She seemed to be lost in thought for a while, trying to piece together the words Jeffrey had said. "This is terrible. How could I have not known this? Where did this happen?"

"Here. She told me it started one night when he came home earlier than expected—the first time was in your bedroom. Then after that, he would wait until you were asleep and go to the basement. She's so worried about you and your relationship. She doesn't want to ruin your marriage."

The tears welled up in her eyes, and as hard as she tried to hold them back, a few wet spots landed on the table. "I'll speak with her," she whispered. "Thank you for telling me. You are a good person, Jeffrey. My sister is so lucky to have you."

He nodded. "I'm sorry to have to be the one to bring you this news, but I couldn't let this go on any longer. Debbie is afraid of him and feels trapped. She thought he was her real friend, so she trusted him until . . . until it got out of hand."

"I need time to register all this. I can't even wrap my head around what you're saying." Laurie shook her head, tears flowing freely now. "I'll get to the bottom of this."

They walked to the front door. Jeffrey hugged Laurie and said, "I know Debbie loves you very much. I hope you guys can work this out."

~ ~ ~

Later that day, I lay in my room, anticipating either a call from Jeffrey or from Laurie. I was praying Jeffrey's call would come first. How could one girl get caught up in so many crazy things in a little over three years? I turned on the radio to hear James Taylor's new song, "You've Got a Friend," playing. All I could think of was, *I need a whole lot more than a friend right now.* I turned over and stuffed my face into my pillow and sobbed until the phone rang. I jumped up.

"Hello," I whispered. My heart sped like a racehorse. I wanted to reign it in, but it was apparently aimed at winning this losing battle.

"Hey, it's Laur." Her voice had a teary-eyed edge to it. "We need to talk. I'll pick you up in twenty minutes."

"Okay," I said, barely able to get out the whole word. *I am not looking forward to this conversation, not one bit.*

I heard Laurie's horn blow. I flew down the staircase, bracing the banister along the way and ending up with burns on the palm of my right hand. I couldn't get my heart rate under control and thought that this must be what it felt like to have a heart attack.

Out the door and into her car I went. I took one look at her face, which was the epitome of sorrow and dread, and slumped down in my seat. I covered my eyes and started to cry again. I rubbed my sleeve to wipe my nose, which was already red and raw from blowing it so much.

"Let's go to the Farm Shop in Amity Shopping Center. We'll talk there."

I nodded.

Once we were in the restaurant, we both ordered a Coke, and then she began with a long list of questions while she swirled the straw around and around in her glass. "How long has this been going on, Deb? Why didn't you come to me? Why didn't you stop it? What were you thinking?"

My head was filled with one big *why*. I wanted her to stop swirling the straw. It was making my stomach feel sicker than it already had. I took a deep breath and started with her first question, hoping I could remember them all.

"About three months. I was deathly afraid to tell you. I was afraid to stop it. I thought if he got upset, he might . . . I don't know. I don't know. I don't have an answer. And, apparently, I *wasn't* thinking, because I let it happen, right?" My sobbing was out of control, and I saw a woman across from us staring. *Fuck off, lady.*

"Try to calm down," she whispered. "Everyone is looking at you. Listen . . . no matter what you did, Harvey knew better. He is an adult. I've already spoken to him, and I told him I've made up my mind: I am going to file for a divorce. Since neither of us wants anyone to know the truth, we will make something up. It's going to be tricky since I'm pregnant. For now, until things are finalized, I think it's better if you don't babysit."

Somehow, through her words, I heard, "Everything is going to work out." I wasn't convinced of it yet, but I had stopped crying. My eyes stung, and I could tell they were very swollen.

I looked down at my Coke, still filled to the top, and said, "I'm so sorry."

~ ~ ~

Not long after the day we talked in the Farm Shop, Laurie filed for divorce, which was finalized approximately a year later. She gave birth to her third child and was now a divorced, single mother of three small children. Harvey had moved out shortly after Laurie had confronted him. She needed me far more than ever to help her with the kids, and I was determined to do just that.

I thought back to a night when I was babysitting and watching the *Mickey Mouse Club* with Laurie's two oldest. I wondered about those Mouseketeers—Karen, Annette, and all the others. Their world looked so innocent on the television screen. What was their life like growing up? Were any of them like me? Damaged or broken by unthinkable things? Yes, I had been damaged and broken, but somehow, I knew deep inside, I was not completely undone. And if that were the case, just like the many sweaters I knitted over the years with precise intricacy, stitch by stitch, row by row, skein by skein, the finished piece would someday be made whole.

Chapter 15

My 1972–1973 desk calendar sat alone in the same spot as the 1969–1970 one did that had "period" written on the day the dam was supposed to break but didn't. Now written was a large "X" with the words "leave for college" on the first of September 1973, an invisible reminder that should have said "leaving for Willimantic—your free get-out-of jail card awaits you here!" This was the day I would move into off-campus housing where I would live while attending Eastern Connecticut State College. It was still months away, but with Jeffrey's help, I had applied to, and thankfully gotten several acceptances to enter several junior colleges as well as Eastern Connecticut State College, even though my SAT scores were far from admirable. *Why did I smoke all that pot in high school?*

Senior year was a breeze, but then again, I walked around high school half stoned, and so even the windiest of days, I delicately danced like feathers floating from classroom to classroom. My homeroom teacher, Barry Hill, was a handsome black man with a stocky build. His demeanor was warm, and his bright smile and snow-drenched teeth stood out quite prominently amid his full beard and mustache. I hadn't spoken with him much during the short homeroom period, but I'd seen him during the day when I was in Ms. Barnes' English class. After seeing him chatting with her on several occasions, I'd guessed that they were an item or connected in some way.

English class with Ms. Barnes was my favorite class that year, and one I shared with Jeffrey. Jeffrey and I did English homework together most days, and once he was done with his, he helped me with mine. I'd pay close attention to his help as he magically made every syllable dance on the paper. I absorbed as much as I could until my mind was soaked. Jeffrey was such a smart boy, and I was one lucky girl to have his guidance.

Ms. Barnes was what I would call a "cool" teacher. She behaved more like a friend than a teacher. I wouldn't describe her as an attractive lady but rather plain-looking, kind of like a bagel without a schmear. I didn't know her age, but if I had to guess, she wasn't much older than me, maybe twenty-three or twenty-four years old. I'd imagined her to be fresh out of college or close to it. There were days I'd stay after class and chat with her while Jeffrey left to go to his part-time job. I loved the charming way she made me feel like a girlfriend instead of a student. The more I hung out with Ms. Barnes after class, the more that all-too-familiar need to feel special surfaced again. Then one day, as if she could read my thoughts, she invited me to her house to hang out on one frigid, bone-chilling November day.

~ ~ ~

"We're here!" Ms. Barnes said as she pulled into her driveway.

"Oh, wow!" I beamed. "You don't live far from me at all. Do you own this house?"

"Nope, this is what they call a two-story flat, and I rent the second story."

When we entered the center doorway to her house, a hallway led to the first-floor flat and a set of very steep stairs led up to hers. When we got upstairs, we walked directly into her kitchen. I had hardly noticed anything as I awkwardly glided behind her as if on ice skates for the first time, my high-heeled boots wobbling at the ankles.

"Sit," she said, pointing to a chair in the kitchen. "I'll make us some hot cocoa." I didn't respond but thought it was the perfect match to the cold, blustering winter day from which I had just come out of.

Her kitchen was small and quaint. The yellow cabinets with turquoise countertops were outdated but still in impeccable shape, especially for a rental. We sat and talked at her kitchen table that sat two, and while we both sipped at our cocoa, Ms. Barnes massaged my mind with compliments, as if she were meticulously preparing the next day's lesson plan. I listened intently to her words, letting them fill me like a deflated tire being pumped full of air. Then a feeling I was acquainted with swept over me. *I've sure had my share of flat tires in the past several years.*

When we were done with the cocoa, she took the cup from me and placed her cup and mine in the sink. When she left the sink, she walked behind me and accidentally—*or was it intentionally?*—brushed her hand lightly across the top of my back. It sent waves down each arm toward my hands, finally exiting through each fingertip. Whatever I felt at that moment was way different than what I had experienced while playing with Laura as a young child. My mind was orbiting around my head, my thoughts spinning out of control. Why did my body respond like that to her touch? Had I enjoyed it?

Snapping out of my thoughts, I heard Ms. Barnes exuberantly say as she walked to one side of me, "Hey, do you get high?"

"I do…" There was an inflection in my voice as if I were asking a question rather than answering one. *This is odd.* Trying to dismiss that somehow, I knew there was more to this question and where this might be heading.

"Well, come with me. I've got some great stuff. Oh, and by the way, call me Linda. Enough with that formal Ms. Barnes crap, at least when we aren't at school."

I followed her into her bedroom, where we sat at the edge of her bed. While she got out her weed and rolling paper, I peered around the room and noticed the pretty and delicately flowered window valences matching the soft Laura Ashley quilt atop her bed. In between two windows sat a small desk covered in neat piles of what appeared to be papers to correct, and above her bed, a large oil painting of a vase filled with abundant flowers—a pleasing contrast to the dainty flowers on the valences and quilt. When she finished rolling the joint, she lit it up and we smoked it until it transformed into the tiniest of roaches, which, by the time we were finished, had also been crawling all over me. I stood up and asked to use the bathroom, scanning my body for those ugly black things. My feet moved, but I could not feel the ground under me.

Wow, I'm so fucking high. I think that stuff is laced with something. I thought I had said that to myself, when Linda blurted out, "Yeah, me too." I was wondering if she heard me or if I was imagining her response.

I made it to the bathroom, and while sitting on the toilet, I placed my head in my hands and repeated in mantra fashion, "What in the world are you doing? What in the world are you doing? What in the world are you fucking doing? Okay, calm down, you are okay. After all, Linda is your English teacher . . . right?"

I could hardly hoist myself off the toilet—my body was stuck to the seat. When I finally unglued myself, I stumbled my way back to her bedroom.

In a very stoned whisper of very slurred words, Linda mumbled, "Come, come lie down next to me." I walked around the bed and flopped down, feeling like a beached whale of ginormous size as the waterbed mattress rippled under me until coming to a slow halt. Linda reached over to me and pulled me along the side of her body. I lay close to her with my head against her chest. The movement from the waterbed settled down while she stroked my hair for what seemed like hours. I could feel myself dozing off when she murmured in my ear, "I have a great idea. Let's take a bubble bath."

"Why not? Let's do it," I murmured back, sounding like a drunken sailor. I tried to get up but fell right back down on the bed. "Okay, let me try that again." I took one big push forward and, without stopping, stumbled around the bed to follow Linda to the bathroom in a conga line of two; neither one of us was steady on our feet.

Singing Joni Mitchell's "Both Sides, Now," Linda danced and pranced around the bathroom, shedding her clothes as I did the same. She turned on the faucet and poured liquid bubbles under the running stream. There, before our eyes, the first bubble was born, and then another and another. Large bubbles and small bubbles, rising bubbles and falling bubbles, growing bubbles and shrinking bubbles, all playfully and gracefully bouncing against each other. I'd never seen so many bubbles in my life. When we finally stepped into the tub and lowered our bodies into the water, bubbles rose until they cascaded over the sides and onto the floor.

After bathing, we dried off and went back to her bedroom. By this time, I knew what was going to happen next, so I abruptly said, "I've never been with a woman before. Well, at least in this way. When I was eight or nine years old, I'd play doctor with my childhood girlfriends, but I don't think I can compare that with this." At that moment, I was a dumb kid and wished I could take back everything I'd said.

But before I could utter another dumb word, Linda covered my mouth with her hand and said, "Relax. It's going to be just fine." And it was.

Women are so much gentler than men, I thought.

After I got dressed, I noticed a slight headache coming on as my high dissipated. I asked Linda for a couple of aspirin, which she promptly retrieved. She offered to drive me home, and even though it was cold, I graciously declined because I needed to clear my head with some fresh air. She walked me downstairs, and out the door, and off I went to the bus stop, where I took the ride home. My mind meandered through the labyrinth of the afternoon; I was pleased that Linda had taught me something other than English that day. I was hoping there would be more days like that, and there were, and much to my surprise, I would learn and experience yet another new thing.

After English class a few weeks later, Linda motioned me to come her way. I walked over, and she said, "Deb, I wanted to tell you the last writing assignment you handed in was a marked improvement from the previous one. Keep up the good work. So, what is it you want to major in?"

"I've volunteered a few times at the rehabilitation center here in New Haven. I have a real passion for working with the disabled. I think special education might be my direction; however, I also love psychology. Hah! If I can learn to understand my mother more, it might be worth minoring in." I chuckled and said, "Or better yet, maybe I can fix her!"

She offered a smile. "That does sound like a plan, Debbie. You are a smart young woman, and I think you can do just about anything you want. Your future looks bright from my perspective. I also see a passion for life in you that I don't see in most of my students. On another—"

I was suddenly lost once again, in Azzie's words from long ago: *"I know in that pretty little blonde head of yours, you can do anything you put your mind to."* I had heard this sort of thing from other teachers too, yet I was still not convinced I could accomplish much. No one in my household had ever sat down to talk about my life or to guide me on how to go about pursuing this so-called bright future. My sisters had already gotten on with their lives, or so it seemed; Annabelle had graduated from junior college and was married with two kids. Laurie had been married, gave birth to three children, and became divorced (oh, yeah, I was responsible for that). Joanne also had been married, also had three children, divorced, and moved back to New Haven to get her life back in order. Both of my brothers were a huge disappointment to my parents—Gary, who had taken up most of my parents' time fighting drug addiction, and Kenny, who had chosen his passion for wildlife and nature. Neither of them fit the Jewish mold. "My son(s) must grow up to be a doctor or lawyer," my mother had announced. I was pretty much on my own to figure out this whole "future" thing. Although I was often trapped in a vortex of uncertainties, I knew—somehow, I just knew—that I would figure it all out.

"Debbie, are you with me?"

Realizing I had spaced out and was still standing there with Linda, I abruptly said, "Yeah . . . sorry about that, I was lost in thought about that 'bright future' of mine."

Linda walked toward the chalkboard. I noticed her shiny, straight, silky hair bob from side to side. I always wanted her kind of hair but instead had thick, coarse, dry, and frizzy hair. I even tried Breck shampoo that claimed they had a formula for dry hair. So as much as I wanted to be a Breck girl, as their advertisement promised, I came up short. Maybe my mother should add "You'll never be a Breck girl" to her list of positives for me, along with the classics: "You're too fat" and "Do something about that pimple."

Linda started erasing the day's lesson from the board and began talking again. "As I was saying…. on another note, and as you might suspect from seeing him chatting with me from time to time, your homeroom teacher, Mr. Washburn, his wife, and I are good friends. They are coming over Saturday afternoon around two to hang out, and we'd all like you to join us. What do you say?"

"Really? They want me to join you?" I walked over to the blackboard and asked, "They know we're friends?"

"I told them. I told them what a great gal you are and how much fun we've been having after school. They'd like to get to know you."

"Okay then, sounds super. Thanks for including me. I'll take the bus over, so I might be a tad early or a tad late."

"No problem, Deb. See you whenever you get there."

~ ~ ~

I spent Friday night with Jeffrey who kept me company while I babysat at Laurie's. I didn't dare tell him about my upcoming plans with Linda, Barry, and his wife because I was able to discern that he might not approve. Plus, I had most certainly *not* mentioned my first-ever lesbian experience with Linda, either. Although lesbianism was coming into the political forefront, it had barely scratched the surface between the inception of the National Organization of Women in 1966 and the modern LGBT civil rights movement in 1969. Lesbianism was still looked at by many as immoral and illegal, and it wasn't until 1973 that the American Psychiatric Association removed lesbianism from its list of mental disorders.

The year was 1972, so technically speaking, Jeffrey might have labeled me as mentally unfit. I was surely not going to take that chance, so I kept this a secret. When Jeffrey asked me if I wanted to hang out on Saturday afternoon, I did just as my dear old mother had taught me, and as I had done so many times before: I told a little white lie and said I had promised to help Kenny with a school project.

I woke up the next morning enthusiastically waiting for 1:00 P.M. to roll around so I could hop on the bus to Linda's, where I would spend an afternoon with her, my homeroom teacher Barry, and his wife, whom I'd not yet met. While showering, I recounted my other teacher experiences as these thoughts whirled around my brain like a Hula-Hoop in perpetual motion. The experiences with Mr. Benedetto and Mr. Kurk were as duplicitous and dubious as a Trojan horse invading a computer; yet this teacher and this time seemed different. Spending time with Linda felt like being with my best friend, the best friend who, on two occasions, had been stripped away from me and snatched from my life. Linda *was* my new best friend, and best friends always have your back no matter what. They are the ones you can tell your deepest secrets to and never hold you hostage in what they believe to be right or wrong.

After showering, I got dressed and made myself a tuna sandwich on rye toast, gobbling it down like a hungry wild beast, barely tasting anything as each huge mouthful made its way down my throat. I was out the door by 1:00 P.M., at the bus stop by 1:15 P.M., and on the bus by 1:30 P.M. The bus let me out precisely three blocks from where Linda lived. I made my way to her house, feeling the warmth of the sun tickle my nose. It was a brisk November day. The prospect of the day paired well with my quick steps, which warmed me inside and out enough to where I was sweating. My heavy wool coat produced so much heat that the cowl-neck sweater I was wearing pasted itself to my upper body. I rounded the corner and onto her street, and there in view was her house. I made my way to the front stoop and rang her bell. Less than a minute later, Linda was at the front door.

"Hi, Deb! Come on up. Barry and his wife are already upstairs."

I followed her up the stairs, and Barry Hill, not looking like the same Mr. Hill I remembered seeing every day in homeroom, stood in Linda's living room. He had on a blue, long-sleeved turtleneck top with blue jeans that sat nicely upon his blue suede New Balance sneakers marked by a large yellow slightly tilted "*N*" on the outer side. He was so collegiate looking, like one of the boys you might see walking around campus at Yale

University. I was taken aback once again by his broad smile, bright-white teeth, and boyish good looks.

"Hi, Debbie," he said, gesturing to the woman beside him. "This is my wife, Joy."

"So nice to meet you." I noticed her Black skin was even lighter than Mr. Hill's, and she had the softest-looking afro I'd ever seen on a woman. She wore penny loafers, bell-bottom slacks, and a colorful striped sweater vest over a white-collared shirt.

Linda joined us from the kitchen with a serving plate filled with an assortment of cheeses and crackers, setting it on the coffee table, which was surrounded by a sofa, a love seat, and a wingback chair. "Everyone have a seat!" And as quickly as she placed the tray down, she left the room. When she returned, she had a pitcher of iced tea and a stack of paper cups. Handing the cups out to everyone, she said, "Help yourself, please."

We sat and ate while Joy asked me a lot of questions about my "bright" future. Barry chimed in at times while Linda was busy rolling a joint, or from the circumference of it, a blunt. We smoked until we were as high as kites, laughing, and enjoying the conversation that quickly bounced from one topic to the other. Before I knew it, Linda led us all into her bedroom where Joy was the first to undress, then Linda, then Barry, and finally me. Trying hard not to stare, I noticed Barry's body had looked a whole lot better with clothes on, his protruded belly merging with his belly button as it disappeared into the folds of his fat.

Joy began and orchestrated the way while the three of us—Joy, Linda, and me—became one. Our bodies twisted in a beautiful communion while Barry, the voyeur, awaited his turn. And when we were all spent, I lay in bed nestled between two teachers and a wife. I wondered in silence and whispered these words under my breath, *What the fuck just happened?*

~ ~ ~

That day was the last I spent time with Linda or Barry and Joy outside of school. It was a fleeting experience due to what I believe was my sister Joanne's discovery of my encounter with them. Although I cannot remember how she found out, I can remember how utterly humiliated I was the day she confronted me. It was as though I was being exposed for crimes I had not committed, and it took me back to that day in her kitchen in 1968. I had often wondered if Joanne acquired my mother's detective-like and uncanny way of keeping an eye on us. I'll probably never know the answer; however, the betrayal I experienced from her prying into my life was something I never forgot. And although I know she was more concerned with my reckless teenage behavior, I believe her approach was wrong. At that time in my life, I had needed more than a slap on the hand, more than being blamed for something I didn't understand was wrong in the first place. Instead, I had needed what I yearned for throughout my life entire life: nurturing, love, guidance, and a sense of self. I needed to understand how a strong, confident, and self-assured young woman, like the one sitting on that easel in Mr. Kurk's studio long ago, could stand up for herself. I needed to understand how, within me, was the strength to keep out the enemy like an impregnable fortress of steel and one that might have—just might have—prevented me from making many poor choices.

Maybe I wouldn't have gotten in the car with Mr. Benedetto.

Maybe I wouldn't have ended up having sex with Mr. Kurk on the floor of art class and in his studio.

Maybe I wouldn't have chosen an action that could have left me sterile or taken my life.

Maybe I wouldn't have driven stoned just two weeks after getting my license, wrecking my car and nearly killing my friend.

Maybe I wouldn't have allowed my sister's husband to take advantage of me.

Maybe I wouldn't have had a lesbian relationship with my English teacher.

Maybe I wouldn't have had sex with my English teacher, my homeroom teacher, and his wife.

I have since moved on from all the "maybes." By the end of 1972, there were still secrets buried, and some yet to be told. Laurie's divorce had taken place that year. The divorce—or more importantly, the *reason* for the divorce—was never discussed until recently when I decided to write this book. When I asked Laurie to help me fill in some of the missing pieces of my past, she surprised me with a letter that she had held on to for forty-six years, which she kept in a box in her closet. The envelope marked "To be given to Debbie upon my death" held the answer. I had forgotten I wrote the letter. Had Laurie not mentioned it to me, it would have stayed in that box of secrets waiting to be exposed, its words holding answers to so much of who that seventeen-year-old had become.

The letter contained words that were locked away in Laurie's mind and tugging at her heart from time to time—words from so long ago that I needed to hear so I could finish my book, but might not have been, as it had been marked "upon her death." I am grateful to Laurie for so many things, but most of all, that she read the letter to me. A letter that she did not intend for me to have in my possession until her passing, and because of this, I will share with you a glimpse of what hearing her words meant to me.

The letter was written after her divorce, and after Linda, Barry, and Joy and all the others I had trusted. The letter was not dated, but the year had to have been 1972. As Laurie read the letter to me, I hit the record button on my tablet and sat with my mouth agape, listening as if an explosion had just torn through me. I heard, as she took me back on a journey that caused me pain and caused pain to others, a journey trapped between right and wrong, between give and take. I turned up the recording volume so as not to miss a single syllable or word of what Laurie was saying because, as Laurie talked, I was experiencing a tug-of-war with my emotions that ripped at me deeply.

The letter was a plea from me, a young girl, clearly confused between wanting forgiveness yet not understanding why forgiveness was needed. My words spoke of God and his magical creation of man and man's ability to love all and be all through the freedom of one's choices. I spoke in a twisted tongue of confusion, not knowing right from wrong. I asked Laurie for forgiveness if I hurt her in any way and shared my love for her. I begged her to accept me back into her life like a sister. I stated that I would never forgive Joanne for having pried into my life. I professed to be "so happy socially," but I knew that wasn't the case. I wasn't happy at all; I was merely an empty vessel that needed to be filled with love and affection, or a failing dam whose holes needed to be plugged, one attempt after another. And those were both temporary fixes, because my vessel emptied quicker than I could fill it, and the dam failed once too many times, for to begin with its foundation was never strong enough.

The letter spoke to me so profoundly. It enlightened me through the words of my younger self that the actions throughout my life had been like a reckless rockfall that plummeted down the side of a mountain, leaving fragments, small and large, breaking free and leaving a void from their once-secured spot. An empty hole that did not understand empathy or how poor choices could inflict hurt and pain on others. I listened to the recording and Laurie's voice as it resonated in the depths of my being. Each replay brought me to a more transparent and more in-depth understanding of that young girl. I lived in my society with my own set of rules. I had erected my own fortress of protection in a world without barriers. I let in the perpetrators I trusted, who had failed me while helping me build the walls and then smashing them into smithereens. And the other adults who had abandoned me—my mother, my sister Joanne—clearly had no idea they had left me out in the world to be chewed up and spit out and stuck somewhere, like hundreds of tiny lonely pieces of gum stuck under a school desk. My mother and Joanne did the best they knew how with the experiences and guidance they had gathered along their journeys. I forgave them both long ago because I knew in my heart that in their way, they loved me.

As screwed up and crazy as the words in the letter sounded, they spoke of my desperate need for love in any form that it was available. And with all the pain and conflict I experienced and welcomed at times, I was still a courageous warrior. I became a survivor because I knew that deep within me lived something more significant and more powerful than any poor choice I ever made. And just like the many knitted pieces I had unraveled and made whole again, my mission would be to do that for myself.

Epilogue

"Open wide," I said as my mouth opened in a broad gesture to mimic what I wanted my six-month-old son, Michael, to do. His tiny mouth stretched open, and I swirled the baby spoon around in a swift motion while making the sound of an airplane until it entered his little mouth. His approval of this familiar game to get an infant to eat tickled him to death. After each clamp down on the spoon, he'd grin from ear to ear, showing off his one dimple.

"Okay, my sweet one. It's time for mommy to go to work." I swooped him up and out of his highchair. I kissed him gently on his nose. Admiring his light-brown, soft curls, I reaffirmed my conviction that he was the cutest baby ever to be born.

I dropped Michael off on the second floor of the three-story building where I lived on the third floor; the building was owned by Helen and Bill

Haskos. Helen, a sweet and kindhearted woman whose Greek cooking spiraled its way up the stairwell daily, had offered to babysit for Michael so I could return to work. Getting back to my career in the insurance industry would help support my husband's income, which alone was not enough to support our household. Mark, my husband, had recently purchased a new business and it would be several years before it became profitable. Besides, Michael was getting older, so I felt better about leaving him with Aunt Helen, which we warmly named her. I was happy to be working again, but I could hardly wait to get home to Michael and the huge smile he presented to me when I walked in the door.

On my way to work that day, I thought how much I had to be grateful for—I was married now and although things did not work out for Jeffrey and me—he gave me hope that good guys exist. I was twenty-six years old and, a mother. *Mother*. I let the word roll off my tongue a few times and the sound linger a bit. I loved being a mother. I had longed to be one from a young age, and after the fucked-up abortion, motherhood could have been a dream and not a reality. I was determined and committed to showing and giving my children enough love to last a lifetime. I read an article that talked about "breaking the cycle" from past experiences so you don't repeat them yourself. The cycle I was determined to break was my children were not going to be absent of a positive and nurturing mother. When I visited my parents, who were getting on in years, my mother would often say, "Stop kissing on him so much. You are going to smother that poor child." Silently I'd say to myself, Yeah, Mom, just like you did to me, but instead, I would turn to her and proudly say, "If I smother him from too much love, well, then I guess he'll just have to live with that, won't he?"

I was grateful that Azzie was never short on love for me. Had I not known what Azzie's unconditional love felt like, not to mention her constant reinforcement that I could do anything to which I set my mind, it might not have been so easy to break the cycle. I was so fortunate and blessed to have her in my life. I made sure I was in touch with Azzie often. I'd pick her up in her neighborhood, which always took me back to that story she told me as a young girl, affirming all that she had told me. She, Michael, and I would have lunch at Chuck's, her favorite luncheonette on Whalley Avenue, where she'd order a fatty corned beef sandwich and a Coke. The smile on her face made her plump cheeks rise in soft puffs that sat just under her eyes and her hearty "um, um, um" after each bite reminded me of how special Azzie was to me.

I pulled up to the Southeast Insurance office, where I had started working just a month before. I parked and headed into the office, making my way to my desk. Before I got there, I could see a balloon peeking above my cubicle walls. *Hmmm, what is about to happen?* When I approached my desk, there sat a bouquet and a large balloon with the word *Congratulations!* I took a seat and opened the card that was attached to the vase. The card read:

> Dear Debbie,
>
> Congratulations on making sales agent of the month.
>
> Signed,
>
> Mr. Miller and Staff

By the time I finished reading the card, Mr. Miller, dressed in his freshly starched shirt and red suspenders, and the entire staff had surrounded me. "Debbie, a job well done! Your first month on our staff and you've exceeded all sales numbers. I'm very proud of you and am ecstatic to have you as a part of our team." Affirming his delight, he placed a hand on my shoulder and applied a slight squeeze.

"Thank you, Mr. Miller. Honestly, this is such a pleasant surprise." Although I knew that I was kicking ass with sales, I had no idea I would make sales agent of the month. A feeling of pride swept over me. I wanted to jump with joy, run around in circles, and then pick up the phone and call Mark, Azzie, and Laurie, but I contained myself.

Mr. Miller continued: "Lunch is on us today. We will all head over to the Italian restaurant across the street at noon. Again, congrats!" He walked toward his office, and the rest of the staff scattered to their cubicles.

The rest of that day, my body worked as if it had been fueled with high-octane gasoline. The adrenaline rushed through me as I set out to break another record. What were the chances I could make sales agent of the month twice in a row? Nah, that was most likely an impossibility, but even if I didn't make it, I would still put in my best effort as I did with every job I held, and that included King Supermarket.

As I drove home from work that day, I pondered my life's journey. I grew up in a house of chaos, one that lacked the parental acumen to rear a family of six successfully. My house, my home became the perfect backdrop for my vulnerability. I walked the wrong path, whether guided or alone, and met my makers who robbed me of my childhood. I ran from the volatile environment of my home and into the arms of those who made me feel special even if for a fleeting moment. On all accounts, I should have given up on life, yet I persevered. I found strength and resilience through my insurance career when I realized that if I worked a job as if it were my own business, I could achieve greatness. Not only could I achieve greatness, but I could also be proud of the woman I had become despite my past.

I never forgot Mr. Ford, the president of the Home Insurance Company and the first employer of my insurance career. His words and encouragement made an indelible mark on me. On my own volition, I had started to move up the corporate ladder at the Home, going from the typing pool to the rating pool during that summer. At that point, I am not sure if I realized the healing power behind my strong work ethics, or how capable we all are of turning adversity around. I know now. I recall the morning Mr. Ford's voice came over my phone's intercom, summoning me into his office.

"Sit down, Debbie. There's something I'd like to discuss with you." Oh, God, please, I thought, not another one of those pep talks . . .

okay, now, get that absurd thought out of your head!

He continued: "You have been with us for less than two months. It's not often that employees such as yourself come along that work as diligently as you do, who are willing to go the extra mile, come in early or stay late if needed. I want to offer you a full-time permanent position here. Before you say anything, I know you are about to head off to your second year of college; however, if you agree to stay on with us, I am willing to offer you thirteen thousand dollars for your first year, a week's paid vacation, and three sick or personal days. I am also ready to send you to insurance school so you can eventually get your underwriting designation and advance to that position when an opening becomes available in the future. Plus," he continued, offering me a polite smile, "you will get a better education here with me, with us, and, after four years here, you will be making more money than you would after graduating at Eastern Connecticut."

"Mr. Ford, I don't know what to say. That is a very generous offer. Can I take a little time to think about it?"

It hadn't taken a few days to make my decision, and by the following day, I had reported to Mr. Ford that I was signing on! That decision, that risky decision to forgo college and risk so much was something that came from a place I hadn't known existed ever before. I had to convince myself that Mr. Ford was not another Mr. Benedetto, Mr. Stein, Mr. Chovnik, Mr. Kurk, or Harvey. I had to reach deep inside me, breaking through the fear, the doubt, and the brokenness until somehow, someway, whether it was God or some other greater power, I found the strength and resilience to rise above it all. There, all along waiting for the right moment was a force more significant than I could have imagined ready to help me lead the way.

    I approached my neighborhood and, by far, the most exciting part of my day. I walked into Helen's kitchen and peeped around the corner into her living room where I would catch that first glance from Michael. His glowing smile and tiny arms stretched as far as he could reach, eagerly waiting for me to lift him up and out of his playpen. A priceless moment. Motherhood filled me with an undeniable feeling of joy and satisfaction. The deep desire to parent had furrowed its way into my being from a young child and now, that desire was finally satisfied in motherhood. Through motherhood, I could give more than I had received, and once and for all, I could break the cycle. And although I knew I'd make mistakes along the way, I was determined to forge a union of love and support with my children that could overcome obstacles along the way.

I knew that moving forward in life, I might encounter challenges surrounding trust, men, and relationships, but I was steadfast in making the best with which I had to work. I made sure I kept Azzie's words alive: "You can do anything you put your mind to. You are a very smart girl." Those words mattered, and therefore I knew, I mattered. Her words pushed me through my landscape of rugged terrain and murky waters that, in the end, led me to fields of colorful blossoms filled with hope and promise. Yes, through it all—through all those who tried to unravel me—through all the misguided promises, through all the wrong choices, I got to do it over—my way, stitch by stitch.

About the Author

Debbie Barnett grew up in New Haven, Connecticut, and now resides in The Villages, Florida. *Innocence Unraveled* is her second published book. Her first book, *Unlocking the Secrets of American Mah Jongg,* is a beginner's guide on how to play Mah Jongg.

In addition to writing, Debbie has a full-time business teaching Mah Jongg through her online school, *School of American Mah Jongg*, a first-time-ever live-interactive classroom for beginners, intermediate, and advanced players.

When she is not working, Debbie enjoys an afternoon of Mah Jongg, playing golf, and spending time with her grandchildren.

She can be contacted online at
www.debbiebarnettauthor.com,
www.facebook.com/debbiebarnettauthor/,
www.instagram.com/debbiebarnettauthor,
or https://twitter.com/DebbieBAuthor

www.ingramcontent.com/pod-product-compliance
Lightning Source LLC
Chambersburg PA
CBHW071225080526
44587CB00013BA/1505